# WHAT YOUR COLLEAGUES ARE SAY

# the Artificial Intelligence playbook

# the Artificial Intelligence playbook

### Time-Saving Tools for Teachers that Make Learning More Engaging

Meghan Hargrave | Douglas Fisher | Nancy Frey

CORWIN

Fisher & Frey

FOR INFORMATION:

Corwin

A Sage Company

2455 Teller Road

Thousand Oaks, California 91320

(800) 233-9936

www.corwin.com

Sage Publications Ltd.

1 Oliver's Yard

55 City Road

London EC1Y 1SP

United Kingdom

Sage Publications India Pvt. Ltd.

Unit No 323-333, Third Floor, F-Block

International Trade Tower Nehru Place

New Delhi 110 019

India

Sage Publications Asia-Pacific Pte. Ltd.

18 Cross Street #10-10/11/12

China Square Central

Singapore 048423

Vice President and
  Editorial Director: Monica Eckman

Director and Publisher: Lisa Luedeke

Associate Content
  Development Editor: Sarah Ross

Product Associate: Zachary Vann

Production Editor: Laura Barrett

Copy Editor: Diane DiMura

Typesetter: C&M Digitals (P) Ltd.

Proofreader: Theresa Kay

Cover Designer: Rose Storey

Marketing Manager: Megan Naidl

Printed in the United States of America

A Library of Congress Cataloging-in-Publication Data record is available for this title.

ISBN 978-1-0719-4963-4

This book is printed on acid-free paper.

24 25 26 27 28 10 9 8 7 6 5 4 3 2 1

# CONTENTS

**Acknowledgments**      xi

**Introduction**      1
     Enter Generative AI      2

## PART 1: ESSENTIALS      7

**CHAPTER 1:** Getting to Know AI .................................9
     Artificial Intelligence Sites for Education      12
     Large Language Model (LLM) Artificial Intelligence      13
     Teacher-Facing Artificial Intelligence      16
     Student-Facing Artificial Intelligence      17
     AI Sites Worth Exploring      18
     Terms to Know      19
     Conclusion      22

**CHAPTER 2:** Writing Prompts and Avoiding Plagiarism .......23
     AI Prompt-Writing Skills      24
     Plagiarism      27
     Responsible Analysis of Output      29
     Credibility      31
     Conclusion      34

## PART 2: WHY AND HOW TO USE AI      35

**Educator Function #1: Managing Content** ......................37
     Artificial Intelligence–Assisted Teacher Functions      38
     Content Generation      39
     Content Organization      41
     Content Revision      42
     Content Consolidation      43
     Conclusion      47

## Educator Function #2: Fostering Student Engagement ............................................. 49

Fostering Background Knowledge ............................... 51

Artificial Intelligence for Relevance ............................ 53

Increasing Choice to Increase Engagement ............... 57

Gamify Learning ............................................................ 59

Making Content Applicable ......................................... 61

Teaching Engagement ................................................. 62

Conclusion ..................................................................... 64

## Educator Function #3: Meeting Students' Instructional Needs ............................................. 65

Artificial Intelligence and Instructional Needs ......... 68

Supporting Language Learning .................................... 74

Adjusting and Customizing Texts ............................... 75

Customizing Scaffolds and Supports ......................... 77

Customizing Interventions .......................................... 78

Conclusion ..................................................................... 81

## Educator Function #4: Assessing Student Learning ............................................................... 83

Developing Assessment Tasks .................................... 86

AI-Resistant Assessments ........................................... 90

Assessments of Transfer ............................................. 92

Interpreting Data ......................................................... 94

Conclusion ..................................................................... 96

## Educator Function #5: Providing Effective Feedback ............................................................. 97

Artificial Intelligence for Feedback ........................... 98

Using AI for Feedback ................................................. 102

Preparing for Student Conferences ........................... 103

Student Exemplar Responses ..................................... 109

Self- and Peer Feedback ............................................. 112

Conclusion ..................................................................... 114

Educator Function #6: Lifelong Learning ........................................... 115

    Clarifying or Refreshing Content Knowledge    119

    Rethinking Instruction    121

    Teacher Coaching and Feedback    124

    New Possibilities    125

    Conclusion    127

**Conclusion**    129

**Appendix**    135

**References**    141

**Index**    143

# ACKNOWLEDGMENTS

Corwin gratefully acknowledges the contributions of the following reviewers:

Alisa Barrett
Director of Instruction
Greenfield, OH

Stephanie Farley
Educational Consultant, Joyful Learning
Studio City, CA

Alejandro Gonzalez
Technology Director, Health Sciences High, and Assistant Professor,
    San Diego State University
San Diego, CA

Carol S. Holzberg
Educational Technology Consultant and Technology Administrator,
    Warwick School District
Warwick, MA

Ruthanne Munger
Writing Specialist, Union School Corporation
Modoc, ID

Darius Phelps
Assistant Director of Programs, New York University
New York, NY

Brett Vogelsinger
English Teacher, Central Bucks School District, CB South High School
Sellersville, PA

Jonathon Walker
Career Technical Education Teacher, Health Sciences High
San Diego, CA

Kim West
Academic Coach and Elementary Math Teacher
Dallas, TX

# INTRODUCTION

For many educators, the new technology came as an unwelcome surprise, particularly for those teachers who were suddenly asked to use it. Many teachers complained about the added work the new technology created for them, and some students refused to comply with the new rules established for it. In fact, the new technology sparked a rebellion of sorts. Some students walked out over the policies. Some students were expelled over it. Yes, in 1830, *when chalkboards were introduced at Yale University,* it was a bumpy road to implementation (Green, 2015). A young man named Alfred Stillé, who eventually went on to become a president of the American Medical Association, was just one of the students expelled from Yale, and there were certainly many others.

When television was introduced into the classroom, educators and family members expressed concern. Some even called it the "electronic chalkboard" or "a numbing substitute for real teaching" (Blubaugh, 1999). The controversy was exacerbated with the introduction of Channel One, a news program that included advertising targeted at youth. In fact, 20 percent of the broadcasting time was spent on ads. Although Channel One was banned in many states, the reach was significant, with millions of students watching daily. Technology that exists in society will permeate schools, and we must learn how to use the tools.

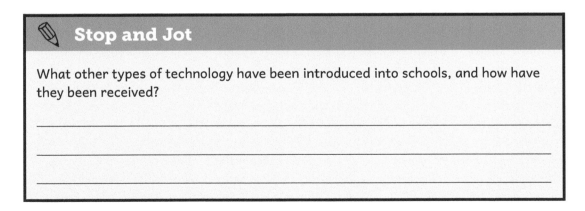

**✎ Stop and Jot**

What other types of technology have been introduced into schools, and how have they been received?

_____

_____

_____

Each innovation in technology requires careful consideration for educators. But, like chalkboards and TV, many popular technological innovations will either be here to stay or will impact what comes down the road. For example, the iPod is no longer widely used but modern smartphones have the features it offered and more. The challenges associated with advancing technologies reminded us of the technology acceptance model (TAM; Venkatesh & Davis, 1996), which suggests there are a range of external variables—including quality of content, utility, price, and design features—which then impact decisions about technology adoption and use. In education, external variables also include the need for new or better instructional strategies and student needs that are not currently being met.

**Figure 1**

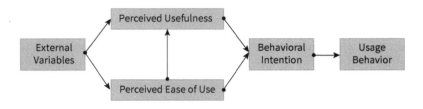

Source: Adapted from Venkatesh & Davis (1996).

The eventual adoption of the technology, whether it be chalkboards, TV, or the internet, is influenced by perceived usefulness and ease of use. In other words, users ask questions like the following: Does it meet a need that I currently have (usefulness)? Can I easily learn how to use it (ease of use)? Is there a reason I must use it (required use)? These variables impact the user's intention, which means the user forms a desire to incorporate the technology because the perception is positive. Our goal in this playbook is to show you not only how to use artificial intelligence (AI) but also how it can meet the instructional needs you have.

## ENTER GENERATIVE AI

It should come as no surprise to readers that our world is experiencing an unprecedented technological revolution. Rapidly changing technologies, specifically artificial intelligence, present an undeniable opportunity to reshape the landscape of education. On November 30, 2022, ChatGPT, the most widely known and used public artificial intelligence chatbot, was launched. It wasn't meant to be made public so quickly, but social media heard about it, and the rest is history (Marr, 2023). Every day educators are learning about new AI sites, and the available tools are multiplying quickly. MagicSchool.ai became the fastest platform in history to reach 1 million users (A. Khan, personal communication, 2024). As the industry undergoes rapid changes, this question arises: Is now the right time to embrace the use of AI in schools? The reality is that although platforms will change and sites will likely become more sophisticated, AI is here to stay, and the impact this technological advancement will have on teachers and students will quite possibly be one of the most positive changes the industry has ever seen (Kahn, 2023).

With the overwhelming pressure for educators to manage a growing list of responsibilities and the stress that comes from these demands, change is imperative. Whether teachers are struggling with time constraints, job responsibilities, lack of materials, the uncertainty of what to use and when, or the impossibility of being an expert in everything, educators face common challenges—and AI is a promising solution. Its ever-growing capabilities and user-friendly interfaces are now making it even easier for teachers and students to learn and grow. AI sites have shown great potential with impressive performance in generating coherent, systematic, and informative content for those who learn to use it effectively (Lo, 2023).

We started exploring the capabilities of some well-known AI sites with fellow educators. Here are some examples of tasks we asked it to manage for us:

- Create middle school–appropriate texts

- Help synthesize student responses into an exemplar essay

- Craft parent communication for conferences

- Generate some games to get eighth graders engaged in math fluency practice

The responses came fast, and the results were impressive. These ideas barely scratch the surface of what AI can offer, but nonetheless, its effective management of these kinds of tasks has left teachers in awe.

It is also important to note that for many teachers, the topic of AI and the pending changes can feel scary. As familiarity and comfort with classroom tools and routines decrease, anxiety increases. It is natural to mourn some of the aspects of the past that have been replaced. When we ask educators to talk about *what was* versus *what is*, they usually identify some of the following changes:

| What Was | What Is |
|---|---|
| Cursive skills | Print and typing skills |
| Long-division algorithm | Ability to explain math reasoning |
| Knowing to indent when paragraphing | Proficient with computer editing tools |
| Familiarity with Shakespeare | Understanding of author's craft and purpose (what authors seek to accomplish and techniques used) |
| Name and date a page | Submit assignments on a learning management system and independently navigate many digital assessment platforms |

That's not to say that handwriting and cursive should be eliminated or that students should not know Shakespeare. It's just that some of those skills that we may have enjoyed teaching in the past, have been evolved into other competences given the technology that exists and the society in which we all live.

As students begin to use AI systems more and more frequently, they will still need to think about the information generated. In fact, critical thinking skills will become increasingly valued as students receive an increasing number of synthetic texts generated by AI systems. They will still need to engage in analysis and interpretation, but inferencing, verbal reasoning, problem solving, and decision making will become major aspects of the curriculum. Reading skills will remain a critical necessity, and students who struggle with this access ability will be increasingly placed at risk as generative AI produces more and more things for them to read and understand. Writing original texts will also be highly valued. In fact, skills for writing prompts for the AI systems, a skill we will address in Chapter 2, are already being taught in schools.

## Ask a Bot

To show how quickly users can obtain information using AI tools, we asked ChatGPT (the free version) to provide a one-sentence summary for third graders about the life cycle of a plant. Instantly, the system responded: *Plants start as seeds, grow into seedlings with leaves, mature into plants with flowers and fruits, and produce seeds that can grow into new plants, completing their life cycle.*

The key is that students must understand the information that is generated. We'll talk about functions and tools of AI later in the playbook, but for now, please note that while searching for information is still a function that we engage in, the tools we use have changed from encyclopedias to search engines on the internet to AI. In this case, the information was customized to the designated audience, third graders, which would not have been possible with an encyclopedia or a generic internet search.

Of course, discerning between effective and less effective ways for teachers and students to use this life-changing technology is essential. The premise of this book is to support educators in the adoption and use of AI by offering practical and impactful strategies for making it a valuable tool in the classroom. Our goal is simple: By engaging in the various interactive components, you will explore the possibilities of AI and get practical ideas on how to use it immediately in your classroom and the classrooms you support.

McKinsey & Company (2020) surveyed more than two thousand teachers in four countries to find out how educators spend their time. As is evidenced in Figure 2, teachers spend a lot of time preparing for lessons, engaging in evaluation and feedback, performing assessments, and completing professional development. On average, according to this data, more than half of the time, teachers are not directly interacting with students.

This playbook is designed for educators, with the specific intention of lightening the load for teachers. In this spirit, we invite you to consider AI as a virtual teaching assistant that can provide support to you. We hope that the tools in this playbook provide teachers with more opportunities to directly interact with their students, which not only is the reward of teaching but also is irreplaceable by a computer.

**Figure 2** • 50 Average Hours' of Working Time per Week for a Teacher

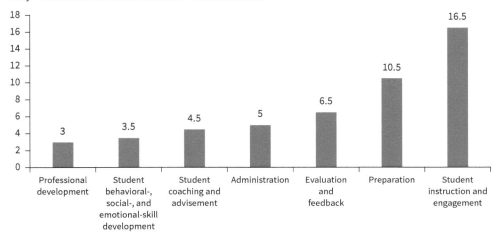

Only 49% of time is in direct interaction with students.

Source: Adapted from Bryant et al. (2020).

To accomplish our goal of increasing the amount of time teachers can spend with students by using AI to accomplish other time-consuming tasks, we have organized this playbook into specific sections that align with the major functions that teachers must accomplish each day:

- Chapter 1 provides an overview of AI in K–12 education.

- Chapter 2 focuses on the issues of plagiarism and citation, which are ethical challenges confronting educators and policymakers; we also share how to create AI prompts that generate useful information.

- Educator Function #1 begins the exploration of functions that AI can assist with by attending to the content that students access based on the standards they are expected to learn.

- Educator Function #2 addresses the issue of student engagement and offers tools to increase relevance and motivation using AI to create and modify learning experiences.

- Educator Function #3 looks at the ways in which teachers can use AI to meet the instructional needs of students, essentially differentiating the experiences without lowering expectations for students.

- Educator Function #4 explores the ways in which teachers can provide feedback for students using AI.

- Educator Function #5 considers the uses of AI in terms of assessment and how evidence is collected from students.

- Educator Function #6 focuses on the need for teachers to engage in continued learning and development as professionals throughout their career.

We generated these topics from the questions we have been asked by thousands of educators about the potential of AI to support teachers to accomplish their work. Importantly, while AI has the potential to reduce the workload for educators, it is not replacing teachers. The growth-producing and caring dynamic between teachers and students remains central to the work we do. It's our *why*. But as you will see in the pages that follow, AI can help with the *how*.

# Essentials

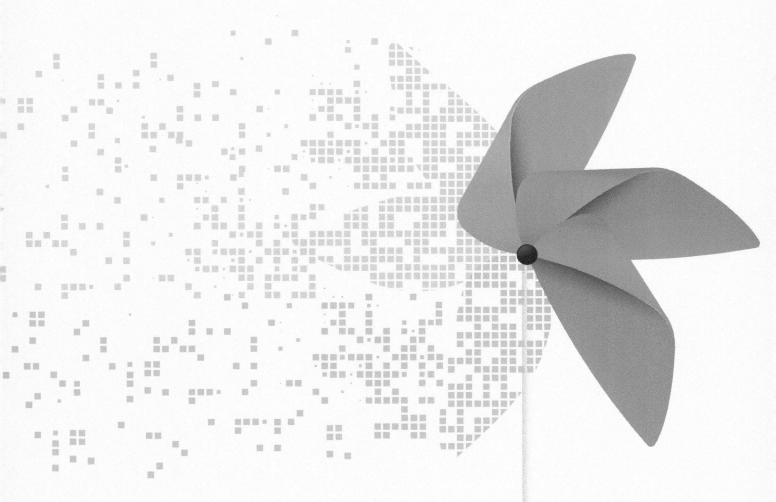

# Chapter

# 1

## Getting to Know AI

**CHAPTER CHALLENGE**

- Try on at least one AI tool and reflect on your emotional response to change, specifically related to the adoption of AI.

Learning any new technology often comes with some initial challenges, and getting started with artificial intelligence is no different. While the learning curve may appear steep, and the tools intimidating at first, we have found that exploring this technology and these platforms with educators has brought a sense of excitement and newfound energy to those who jump in and try it out. The technology is ever-changing, and its capabilities seem limitless—which means that no manual or set of directions will beat exploring and discovering on your own. The goal of this chapter is to help you do just that. See this as a starting point and a launchpad for all the possibilities to come.

### Stop and Jot

Where are you in the AI journey?

_____

_____

_____

Is AI new to you?

1   2   3   4   5   6   7   8   9   10

1 (completely new)          10 (not new at all)

*(Continued)*

(Continued)

What aspects of AI's potential for assisting educators intrigues you the most?

_____

_____

_____

What concerns or reservations do you have regarding the use of AI in supporting educators?

_____

_____

_____

Of course, as you get to know this technology while engaging in this playbook or as you continue to explore AI on your own, you'll likely experience a range of emotions and feelings toward it. We believe the Kübler-Ross Change Curve, first created in the late 1960s to help capture the stages associated with change, accurately captures the trajectory of what educators have felt toward AI when working with it for the first time (see Figure 3).

**Figure 3 •** The Kübler-Ross Change Curve

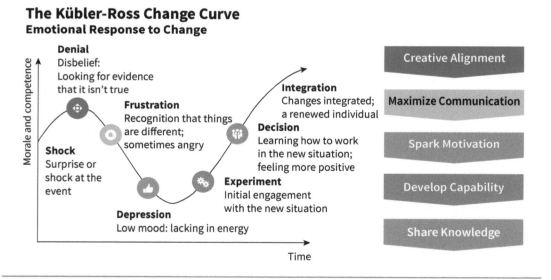

**The Kübler-Ross Change Curve**
**Emotional Response to Change**

Source: The Kübler-Ross Change Curve® is an adaptation of The Five Stages of Grief® from ON DEATH AND DYING by Elisabeth Kübler-Ross®. Copyright ©1969 by The Elisabeth Kübler-Ross Family LP. Reprinted by arrangement with The Elisabeth Kübler-Ross Family LP and The Barbara Hogenson Agency, Inc. All rights reserved. Elisabeth Kübler-Ross®, The Five Stages of Grief ® and The Kübler-Ross Change Curve® are Registered Trademarks.

Each of these stages highlight valid and appropriate emotions to have as you confront the change. We encourage you to remain open to possibilities, to let the suggestions in this playbook spark your own imagination and creativity, and to embrace a "think outside the box" mentality. Try to set aside thoughts about how you have always done things and any self-imposed roadblocks as to why it might not work. Know that even as you are reading, the technology is getting better with regular software updates, the introduction of new features, and improvements that are making platforms more accessible to users. We can only begin to imagine the capabilities of how AI can and will support K–12 educators worldwide.

## ✎ Stop and Jot

What stage in the change model are you experiencing?

_____

_____

_____

Where would you like to be?

_____

_____

_____

How might you get there?

_____

_____

_____

## Task Takeover

### Exploring Possibilties

Let's try a task with AI. Visit the ChatGPT website https://chat.openai.com. Let's imagine that you've been thinking of alternative ways to take attendance, but you don't want to use higher-end technology tools in your classroom to do so. Type this prompt in the message box: *Nontechnological methods that teachers can use to take attendance.*

Look at the ideas that are generated. Some are likely known to you such as having students submit their assignments or checking their name on a list at the door. But are there any that you might use, even episodically, to take attendance differently? In this case, AI generated ideas. In the future, this feature will focus on the ways that AI can do a task for you. In terms of attendance, facial recognition is coming, and students will probably check in with smartphones in the near future. In addition, voice recognition and biometric scanning may soon replace the systems we use to take attendance.

Artificial intelligence itself refers to the ability of machines to do human-like tasks and engage in human-like conversation. Some of the most popular sites are not specific to education, but they can still help with teacher tasks if you use the right prompts. These sites, referred to as large language models (LLM), have access to a deep well of data (as vast as the internet itself) to help them engage in tasks prompted by the user. Though the sky's the limit on what they can offer, they require the user to practice a certain level of thinking, creativity, and prompt generation in order for the information produced to be relevant and effective.

Other sites are designed for a specific purpose or user. Those sites offer a variety of features, usually called *tools,* that guide users to input certain information needed for the resource the sites will create. There is value in educators exploring a wide variety of sites, knowing that different sites might offer help for different topics. To help you get started, we will explore specific sites in the next few sections.

## Self-Assessment

The following list of potential AI uses will expand over the course of this playbook. For now, use the scale to identify some of the ways that AI may be able to help you (blue is good or regularly; orange is the opposite). What areas do you want to strengthen?

| Menu of Potential Uses of AI | |
| --- | --- |
| Writing grade-level examples | |
| Planning lessons and units | |
| Creating student feedback | |
| Translating texts and directions | |
| Creating math word problems and rich math tasks | |
| Adding visuals to text | |
| Making lessons into games | |
| Changing readability levels | |

## ARTIFICIAL INTELLIGENCE SITES FOR EDUCATION

In the sections that follow, you will find we have mentioned some AI sites we found particularly helpful at the time of publication. If you haven't visited the sites before, you will need to create an account to start access. Many of the sites suggested have free access for initial use. Keep in mind that the list of available AI sites is rapidly growing and changing. We hope that our discussion of the general types of sites and the function or use of each will help you gain clarity about the AI process and its potential regardless of your ability to connect with the specific site itself.

# LARGE LANGUAGE MODEL (LLM) ARTIFICIAL INTELLIGENCE

As we noted earlier, LLM sites are the most widely used AI tools that allow users to shape the direction of the interaction. When you first engage with their open-ended features, the process may remind you of starting a Google search. As with Google, you will input a question or request (referred to as a *prompt*) and receive a response. However, unlike Google, these models don't present a list of websites for you to independently explore. Instead, they offer an answer or a suggestion, initiating a response for you that is similar to a human interaction or conversation.

When you prompt the chatbot, you can continue a back-and-forth discussion (which we will refer to throughout this playbook as a *back-and-forth*) to seek additional information, to gain clarification, or even to debate its replies, much as you would when having a live conversation with a peer or colleague. LLM platforms, also sometimes referred to as *generative AI tools*, use natural language processing to understand and generate human-like conversation (Lo, 2023). Though AI pulls its information from the internet, it is also able to generate and create in ways that go well beyond the current capabilities of a search engine.

## Try It Out!

### Search Engines vs. Large Language Models (LLMs)

Step 1: Decide on a topic you want to research.

Step 2: Visit a search engine like Google.com and enter a request in the search field. Consider the following questions:

- What responses does it give?
- Where is it pulling information from?
- Did it give you the information you needed?
- What else would you want to know?

Step 3: Visit a large language model (LLM) AI site like ChatGPT (chat.openai.com), and enter the same request. Consider the following questions:

- How is a chatbot response different from the search engine response?
- Does the reply match what you were looking for?
- If this reply was shared by a human, what would you say back?

*(Continued)*

(Continued)

Step 4: Engage in some dialogue with the LLM site. We recommend at least four or five interactions to get a sense of what it can offer. Consider the following replies:

- Explain more.

- I don't understand _____. Give me an example.

- What would this mean for _____?

- *What else do I need to know about this topic?*

Step 5: Compare and contrast the sites. What do you notice about the difference in capabilities of search engines versus artificial intelligence?

Here's our example. We wanted to know about the benefits of technology in the classroom, so we typed "what are the benefits of technology in schools" into Google, which generated a list of about 733,000,000 sites in 0.41 seconds. That's both impressive and overwhelming. Like other search engines, Google uses an algorithm that evaluates several factors to assess the relevance, authority, and user experience of a website; the algorithm then generates the top results (see Figure 4). Our responsibility as users is to filter through the information and make decisions about what is useful. Like our students, we tend to visit only the top few sites to see what they have to offer.

**Figure 4** • Google Search for "What Are the Benefits of Technology in Schools"

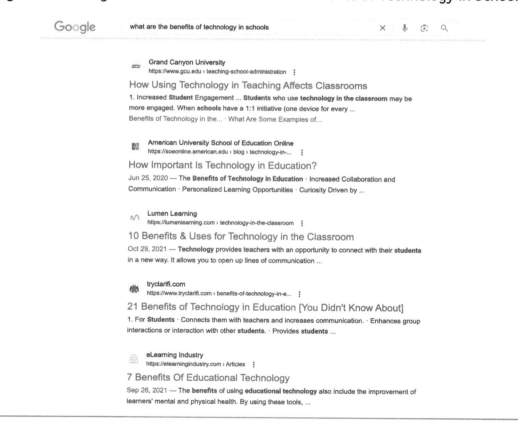

We entered a similar prompt into ChatGPT and obtained much more concise information (see Figure 5).

**Figure 5** • ChatGPT Request for "Explain the Benefits of Technology in Schools in Four Sentences"

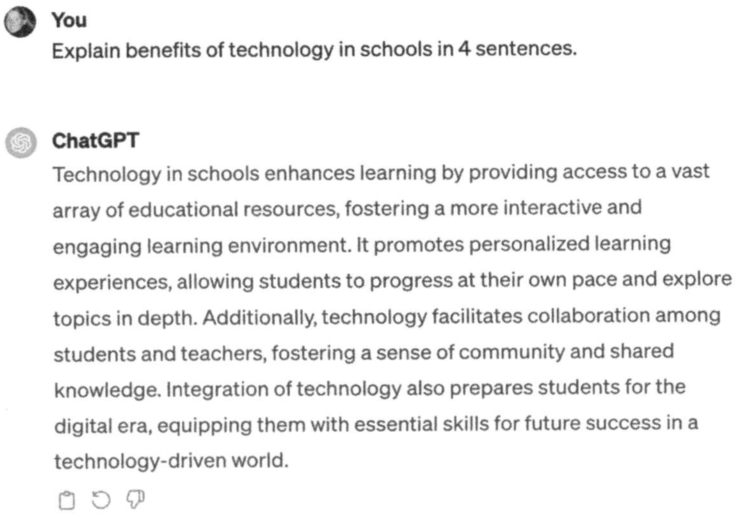

**You**
Explain benefits of technology in schools in 4 sentences.

**ChatGPT**
Technology in schools enhances learning by providing access to a vast array of educational resources, fostering a more interactive and engaging learning environment. It promotes personalized learning experiences, allowing students to progress at their own pace and explore topics in depth. Additionally, technology facilitates collaboration among students and teachers, fostering a sense of community and shared knowledge. Integration of technology also prepares students for the digital era, equipping them with essential skills for future success in a technology-driven world.

Source: ChatGPT.

The information is summarized for us. It's organized into blocks of information. It's understandable and the synthesis is clear. But note that there are no sources cited. This information was gathered from somewhere, but it's impossible for users to know where. At the time of publication, ChatGPT is only accessing information through 2022. That will change as the technology grows, but from what we know now, AI tools do not always have the most up-to-date-information. Consequently, it's important to note that there are inherent risks with using generative AI, which is why there are policies and procedures being developed to protect intellectual property and users of these systems.

---

## Ask a Bot

We asked ChatGPT about the risks that come when educators use generative AI. The system not only gave a quick response, but also provided a thorough one: "While Generative AI has the potential to offer valuable tools for educators, there are also several risks and challenges associated with its use. It's important for educators to be aware of these potential pitfalls to ensure responsible and effective implementation" (OpenAI, 2024). Some of the risks it listed included the following:

- Bias and fairness

- Quality of output

*(Continued)*

> (Continued)
>
> - Overreliance on technology
> - Accessibility
> - Privacy and security
>
> ChatGPT went on to explain more about each category.
>
> What we found most interesting was that the technology was not overly complimentary of its capabilities and gave an honest and complete response about how the source itself has limitations. We will address some of these concerns in the chapters that follow; we also encourage you to go to the source itself when you have concerns. Ask it questions like these:
>
> - *What are your limitations with _____?*
> - *What else should I do to make sure _____ is trustworthy?*
> - *What are the different perspectives users have about _____?*

## TEACHER-FACING ARTIFICIAL INTELLIGENCE

In the spring of 2023, as we introduced teachers to AI's capabilities, specifically the use of LLM platforms, we encountered similar questions and comments from educators: "How do you know what to ask?" and "When I asked _____, I did not get what I was looking for." The open models offer many possibilities, and they require the creativity and savviness of the user to provide a prompt that is just right for the query. As we used AI more frequently ourselves, we decided to save prompts that helped us arrive at what we were looking for. By reusing or modifying these prompts, we eliminated the need to reinvent the wheel each time.

As people have started to recognize the possibilities for AI in education, platforms have emerged that streamline the prompt writing process. Sites like MagicSchool.ai, Diffit.ai, and Eduaide.ai were launched at the start of the 2023–2024 school year and have proven useful in helping educators imagine the possibilities of using AI all while reducing the work that goes into open-ended prompt generation. They offer a more structured approach to prompting, giving users specific categories of information to enter such as grade level, standard, assignment, or text. Behind the scenes, these platforms quickly generate a prompt and can output exactly what an educator is looking for. They simplify the process.

Because they are focused on the specific functions, tasks, and needs of educators, teacher-facing artificial intelligence sites are a game changer. It is also important to recognize that teacher-facing sites are rapidly changing. In fact, while exploring one of these sites with a group of Chicago fourth-grade teachers, we saw an update of the site's organization and new tools added. Teachers have also noted that these sites have improved over their short lifespan including additions such as the ability to do the following:

- transfer AI generated content into Google Classroom

- create new and engaging classroom resources like customized *Jeopardy!*

- produce student-facing rubrics specific that seamlessly merge assignments and standards

## Try It Out!

### Getting to Know Teacher-Facing AI Sites

Step 1: Visit a teacher-facing AI site such as MagicSchool.ai or Eduaide.Ai.

Step 2: Create an account, if needed, and log in.

Step 3: Decide on one tool explore.

Step 3: Input the necessary information into the provided fields.

Step 4: Generate results.

Step 5: Try using the responses and additional features to explore its capabilities beyond the prompt itself.

Step 6: Repeat with another feature.

Step 7: Reflect on the ways that this could reduce some of the time you spend on these tasks.

## STUDENT-FACING ARTIFICIAL INTELLIGENCE

Although the primary audience of this playbook is the teacher, each section features ideas for how educators can teach students to use artificial intelligence in productive and ethical ways. Just as there has been an influx of AI tools specifically dedicated to teaching, there are also AI sites primarily created for the use of the student. Many of these sites allow teachers to create assignments and tasks for students to make the most of the technology.

Though some AI features might be new to students, the use of technology, specifically AI, is not. From a young age, most students have talked to Siri and Alexa, and most are accustomed to letting computers and smartphones help them fix spelling errors, type the right word, and even end a complete thought.

Student-facing sites like Socrat.ai and Brainly.com offer features specific to student learning. Teachers can assign students to engage in a debate with a chatbot on Socrat.ai; they can also assign exam reviews on tutoring-style sites like Brainly.com. In some ways, these sites make learning accessible to students who might be too timid to engage in class discussion or do not have access to a tutor or support system at home when doing homework. The reality is that students will be engaged with AI in their near futures, and many already are, and they need to learn how to use this technology in ethical ways that support their learning.

## Class Connection

### Getting to Know Student-Facing AI

Step 1: Visit a student-facing AI site such as Socrat.ai or Brainly.com.

Step 2: Decide on a current topic you are teaching your students, and think about what you want them to engage in. Here are a few options to consider:

- Discourse
- Debate
- Review
- New learning
- Other _____

Step 3: Using tools provided on the student-facing site, create an assignment that will help students practice the content and activity decided above.

Step 4: Try it out as if you were the student.

Step 5: Think about the results and decide if revisions are needed. Consider the following questions:

- Does the assignment created help students practice what I want them to practice?
- Will my students be able to engage with the tools provided on this site?
- Is there a way the assignment could be more specific?

## AI SITES WORTH EXPLORING

Here is a list of the sites we have been exploring for use by educators. Naturally, it is an ever-growing and changing list. We hope this is the start for your exploration, not the end.

Large Language Model AI

- *Bard*: LLM from Microsoft that uses open-ended prompting
- *ChatGPT.ai*: LLM from OpenAI that uses open-ended prompting
- *Claude.ai*: LLM from Anthropic that uses open-ended prompting

Teacher-Facing AI

- *Briskteaching.com*: Chrome extension teachers can use to provide various levels and types of feedback on student work in Google Classroom

- *Curipod.ai*: Lesson-planning tool that integrates multiple mediums

- *Diffit.ai*: Content-generation tool for teachers

- *Eduaide.ai*: Tools and prompts specific for teacher function, including gamifying lessons, creating choices boards, etc.

- *Educationcopilot.com*: Unit and curriculum planner

- *Gamma.app*: Design tool dedicated to formatting presentations and instantly creating slide decks off of content provided

- *Learnt.ai*: Tools and prompts specific for teacher function, largely focused on resources that support planning and productivity

- *MagicSchool.ai*: Tools and prompts specific for teacher function, including report card comment generator, multiple-choice question generator, text-dependent question generator, etc.

Student-Facing AI

- *Brainly.com*: AI-powered tutor meant for students and caregivers

- *Briskteaching.com*: Chrome extension students can use to get different types of feedback on work produced in Google Classroom

- *Consensus*: Tool that acts as a research assistant, merging features of a basic search-engine and generative AI

- *Khanmigo*: AI-powered tutor knowledgeable in wide range of K–12 topics and courses

- *MeetGeek.ai*: Recording tool, originally designed for professional use, that can transcribe and summarize lectures, teaching content, or student conversation

- *Packback.co*: AI-powered writing assistant, with some features that are also useful for teachers

- *Parlay.ai*: Tool that facilitates, tracks, and measures written and verbal discussion

- *Socrat.ai*: Tool designed to foster student discussion

Other Powerful AI Sites

- *Audiopen.ai*: Tool that turns recorded audio into coherent composition

- *CanvaMagicWrite*: Design site that allows users to add images and videos to text and vise-versa.

- *Draftback*: Chrome extension that timelines (and plays back) the writing process of a Google Doc; can be used for students to reflect on writing process and for detection of AI generated text copied onto an assignment

- *TeachFX.ai*: Coaching tool focused on student or teacher talk

# TERMS TO KNOW

In the early pages of this book, or in your initial exploration of AI, you have likely encountered several words and phrases specific to the field. Below is a list of useful definitions for the terms we feel will be most important for you to know as you delve into understanding how AI can benefit educators. We suggest marking this page and using it as a glossary as you engage with the chapters that follow.

- **AI detection:** Tools that attempt to detect the use of AI on a body of work

- **algorithm:** Set of rules or steps followed to get to particular solution

- **applications:** Programs designed to perform certain tasks

- **artificial intelligence:** Technology programmed to think and learn just like humans

- **augmented learning:** integrating technology to enhance a learning experience

- **beta:** Indicates that something is open to use but still in test, or trial, mode

- **bias:** Unfair or prejudiced preferences in data algorithms or output

- **chatbot:** A computer designed to have conversations with human users

- **coding:** Human instructions written in a way that can be read by a computer

- **copilot:** In technology, this refers to a tool or system that assists the user

- **generative AI:** Artificial intelligence technology that can create new content (images, text, music, etc.)

- **guardrails:** Policies or restrictions used to be sure AI handles data responsibly

- **hallucinations:** AI-generated output that is not accurate or does not make sense

- **human-in-the-loop:** The necessity of incorporating human intelligence with an automated system

- **Large Language Models (LLM):** Systems that can process and generate human-like language

- **Personally Identifiable Information (PII):** Data or input that could identify a specific individual

- **platform:** The system, a combination of software and hardware that operates a certain technology

- **prompt:** The skill of crafting strong prompts—human-written requests, directions, questions, or cues for AI—is crucial

- **synthetic content:** Content (text, video, audio, etc.) generated by AI that appears similar to human-generated material

## Check for Understanding

We end each chapter using AI's assistance to create an assessment that will help you review the content of the chapter and check for understanding. The teacher-facing AI sites mentioned throughout this playbook have features that can assist you with creating classroom assessment items, including multiple-choice questions, matching questions, true/false questions, fill-in-the blank questions, discussion prompts, and scenario-based questions. In each chapter, we vary the check for understanding section to show you one of these tools in action. See Appendix for answers to all Check for Understanding questions.

Here are five multiple-choice questions about Chapter 1: Getting to Know AI.

Question 1: What does the Kübler-Ross Change Curve, as mentioned in the chapter, aim to capture?

  a)  Emotional response to change

  b)  Development of technology

  c)  History of AI

  d)  Ethical concerns of AI

Question 2: What is the primary purpose of large language model (LLM) artificial intelligence tools?

  a)  Present a list of websites for independent exploration

  b)  Generate and create human-like content

  c)  Offer step-by-step directions for various tasks

  d)  Act as a search engine

Question 3: What is the function of teacher-facing artificial intelligence sites?

  a)  Platform for student interactions

  b)  Educator assistant for creating engaging resources and generating content

  c)  An easily accessible bank of lesson plans

  d)  Tool for storing student data

*(Continued)*

(Continued)

Question 4: What is the primary audience of this playbook?

a) Parents and caregivers

b) Educational policymakers

c) Members of the public

d) Teachers and leaders

Question 5: What does the term *guardrails* refer to in the context of AI, as mentioned in the chapter?

a) Policies or restrictions used to ensure AI handles data responsibly

b) The system that operates AI technology

c) Human intelligence incorporated with an automated system

d) Programs designed to perform certain tasks

## CONCLUSION

Did you accomplish the challenge? If so, congratulations. If not, there's still time to try on at least one AI tool. And if your emotional response is still at the level of shock, denial, or frustration, hang in there with us. Remember that author and futurist Isaac Asimov said, "I do not fear computers. I fear the lack of them." The absence of these tools could lead to missed opportunities, stalled progress, and the lack of solutions to complex problems—so let's roll up our sleeves and dive in.

# Chapter

# 2

# Writing Prompts and Avoiding Plagiarism

Despite the enthusiasm around AI and its potential, there is still a feeling of "proceed with caution" for some. When mentioning AI to educators, there are mixed responses but almost always we hear some of the following:

- Am I allowed to use that?

- Isn't this a bad thing for education?

- This is scary.

- How do I know this information is true and unbiased?

The apprehension is not solely due to the shock factor in terms of all that AI can do; it is also fueled by the unease associated with the content it generates. According to a 2023 meta-analysis on ChatGPT, some of this concern comes from its unique ability to answer questions, complete writing, and even complete assignments or exams on behalf of a user (Lo, 2023). Taking time to learn how to ethically engage with AI in productive ways, how to avoid plagiarism, and how to thoughtfully analyze the output is essential. This approach starts with getting good information from these systems, which requires writing effective prompts. We will be covering all these essential aspects throughout this chapter.

As responsible users of AI, it's important to be critical of its output. Biases can persist in AI despite its human-like abilities. In fact, AI can reflect the biases that already exist in the world. We must remain vigilant in ensuring the accuracy and objectivity of the information it produces.

---

✎ **Stop and Jot**

Are you nervous about anything related to AI? If so, what?

_____

_____

_____

_____

Have any of your students submitted AI-generated work without including an attribution of their sources?

_____

_____

_____

What do you need to add to the curriculum to ensure the ethical use of AI?

_____

_____

_____

_____

---

## AI PROMPT-WRITING SKILLS

When teachers and students use the various AI models, there is a direct correlation between the quality of the input and the resultant quality of the output. The skill of crafting strong prompts—human-written requests, directions, questions, or cues for AI—is crucial. In this rapidly evolving technological revolution, mastering the art of communicating with AI systems is quickly becoming an essential skill. The more proficient users are at asking for what they are looking for, presenting the prompt request in a way that the computer understands, the more likely they are to get what they want.

Consider human interactions for comparison. After all, AI is meant to engage users in a human-like exchange to get a desired response. If you ask a colleague for a science experiment without providing additional details, you'll receive whatever your colleague infers that you need. On the other hand, if you ask for an experiment related to specific content and include a list of materials, you're more likely to receive a tailored and relevant suggestion.

## Self-Assessment

*Write a prompt that you might use to solicit information from an AI system. Use the scale to assess the quality of the prompt. What areas do you want to strengthen?*

| Aspects of Quality Prompts | |
| --- | --- |
| Specificity. Was the prompt specific enough to solicit information? | ●————————————● |
| Direction. Did you tell the system what you wanted rather than ask a question? | ●————————————● |
| Context: Did you provide context or the why of the request? | ●————————————● |
| Length: Did you tell the system about how long you expected the response to be? | ●————————————● |
| Format: Were you clear about the format of the output you needed? | ●————————————● |
| Inclusion and Exclusion Criteria: Were you clear about what you do want and what do you not want? | ●————————————● |
| Creativity: Did you allow your creativity to shine? | ●————————————● |

Some of your prompt-writing skills will develop over time with repeated use and experience, including trial and error. (Remember how you learned to write search engine queries.) And in the future, AI itself will become more sophisticated in being able to predict what users are seeking. For now, here are some of the aspects we have found to be particularly helpful when writing prompts for AI.

- *Specificity:* As needed, include information about grade level, type of student, standard, time dedicated to the task, and materials to use to help AI give an output that is the closest match to what you are looking for.

- *Direction:* Some of the best prompt-writing advice we got early on was, "Tell, don't ask." Instead of asking AI questions in the same manner as you might approach Google, input a specific set of directions that it can follow. A strong prompt names a precise request and make use of the capabilities of this technology in its ability to surpass a question/answer format.

- *Context:* Providing background information will lead to a reply that better matches the request. In your prompt, include the "why" behind your request, using phrases like

   "I am asking this because . . ."

   "I need this to help students who are . . ."

   "I will use this with or when . . ."

   "This is an assignment meant to . . ."

   "I am a ____-grade teacher, helping students with ____."

- *Length:* When you are inputting a request from AI, you probably have a sense of what you are looking for. Giving specific directions around the length of the response is an important part of prompt writing. You might ask for a certain number of paragraphs, problems, or steps.

- *Format:* If you have a preferred format for the output, include that information in the prompt. For instance, you should specify whether you are requesting a passage, bulleted list, table, or T-chart. Be explicit about your expectations, and the technology will respond accordingly.

- *Inclusion and Exclusion Criteria:* In the prompt, minimize the need for multiple revisions by explicitly stating elements you want included or excluded in the reply. Imagine potential outcomes as you write the prompt, such as "I would like it to include . . ." or "I would like to avoid including . . ." This approach will contribute to more precise results.

- *Creativity:* When writing a prompt, keep in mind that you are inviting the human-like technology to think with and for you, including thinking outside the box. To allow AI to help your own creativity shine, start prompts with phrases such as these:

"Give me ideas for _____."

"Help me imagine a new way of doing _____."

"What other ideas do you have for _____?"

## Try It Out!

### Playing with Prompts

Step 1: Visit your favorite chatbot on an OpenAI site.

Step 2: Enter the following prompts (or similar versions) sequentially. As you read the outputs, notice the differences.

1. Write a story.
2. Write a story at a third-grade level.
3. Write a story at a third-grade level that uses dialogue and description of actions, thoughts, and feelings to develop events.
4. Write a story about a class of San Diego students who visit the zoo. Write it at a third-grade level that uses dialogue and description of actions, thoughts, and feelings to develop events. Make the example a paragraph long.
5. Write a story about a class of San Diego students who visits the zoo. Write it at a third-grade level that uses dialogue and description of actions, thoughts, and feelings to develop events. Make the example a paragraph long and avoid adding words that do not sound like words a third-grade student would use.

Step 3: Reflect on the differences in AI-generated responses. How was the response different with each prompt?

Step 4: Make a list of important reminders when prompt writing.

1. _____.
2. _____.
3. _____.
4. _____.

## PLAGIARISM

*Plagiarism* is the act of taking someone else's original work or ideas and presenting them as your own. Typically, by the upper-elementary grades, students taught how to avoid plagiarism by learning to credit sources and use strategies to state things in their own words. We teach students that plagiarism is not only ethically wrong but can result in serious consequences, ranging from a zero on an assignment to expulsion from school. It is no wonder that this is one of the most talked about concerns with the use of AI in education. Since AI is technically creating a unique human-like response, using extensive data and algorithms to do so, it creates blurred lines for what use of the content it generates is or is not plagiarism.

After working on the paragraph above, we went to AI for some assistance. Here is the prompt and writing we entered.

 **You**

Is the writing clear? Is there anything I should change? I am writing about AI and plagiarism for an audience of teachers learning to use AI in the classroom.

Plagiarism is the act of taking someone else's original work or ideas and presenting them as your own. Typically, by the upper elementary grades, students taught how to avoid plagiarism by learning to credit sources and use strategies to state things in their own words. We teach students that plagiarism is not only ethically wrong but can result in serious consequences, ranging from a zero on an assignment to expulsion from school. It is no wonder that this is one of the most talked about concerns with the use of AI in education. Since AI is technically creating a unique human-like response, using extensive data and algorithms to do so, it creates blurred lines for what use of the content it generates is or is not plagiarism.

 **ChatGPT**

Your writing is clear and addresses a relevant concern about AI and plagiarism in education. However, you can make a few revisions for clarity and emphasis. Here's a revised version:

Plagiarism, defined as the act of presenting someone else's original work or ideas as one's own, is a critical concept in education. Typically, by the upper elementary grades, students are taught how to avoid plagiarism by learning to credit sources and employ strategies to express information in their own words. We emphasize to students that plagiarism is not just ethically wrong but can lead to severe consequences, ranging from receiving a zero on an assignment to expulsion from school.

The integration of AI into education has sparked heightened discussions, and one of the primary concerns revolves around plagiarism. AI, with its ability to generate unique, human-like responses through extensive data and algorithms, blurs the lines between what constitutes original content and potential plagiarism. Teachers navigating the use of AI in the classroom must grapple with the challenge of distinguishing between authentic student work and AI-generated content.

Source: Created with ChatGPT.

Although we decided to keep the writing as is, would using the revised version cross the line of claiming work we did not solely create as our own? In this case, we do not think so. The original content was our own, and we used this AI tool (with our own prompting) to get feedback via a revised version. However, it does give some food for thought and it requires careful consideration when using AI in classroom instruction.

For years, teachers and educational institutions have used plagiarism detection sites trained to flag material that is not the original work of the writer. In fact, most older students have grown accustomed to requirements of running a paper through detection software before turning it in. Many educators also hoped that these sites would flag an overreliance on AI. However, the more sophisticated the AI tools become, the less likely they able to be flagged by plagiarism detection tools.

In a 2023 study, Weber-Wulff and colleagues examined twelve plagiarism detection tools for their ability to flag AI-generated content accurately and reliably. They found that none of the twelve tools were above 80 percent in accuracy, and only five of those were above 70 percent. The authors also reported that the amount of false positives (human-generated content inaccurately labeled as machine-generated) is especially problematic. The tools are also imprecise, and they report only a percentage without identifying specific passages (e.g., "14% likely comes from GPT-3, GPT-4, or ChatGPT"). "Therefore," the authors state, "a student accused of unauthorized content generation only on this basis would have no possibility for a defence" (p. 26).

Though the detection tools educators have used in the past might not be the answer, there are some digital tools and apps we have found to help. For instance, the Google extension Draftback offers a visual replay and a timeline of a document's creation. It has features that allow users to identify instances where large portions of text were copy and pasted or when the content was generated in an unusually short time frame.

So, even with tools like Draftback in mind, what does this mean for educators? Simply banning the use of AI will not work. Instead, teaching students how to use AI responsibly by modeling and practicing ways to use AI while maintaining the integrity of original work is essential. In addition to teaching students how to avoid plagiarism, we might also think about the assignments and tasks themselves: Does this assignment encourage original thought? Does this assignment bring in student critical thinking skills? Could changes be made to this assignment to make the work students have to produce AI-resistant? In Chapter 6, when we look more closely at assessment, we will explore more around this concept.

## Classroom Connection

### Teaching Students About Plagiarism

Using AI with students in the classroom offers a great opportunity to teach learners about plagiarism. Instead of providing students with a list of what they cannot do when it comes to using the work of another author or AI system, teach them what they *can* do. For this we suggest leaning on the work of Vosen (2008), who suggests a sequence of four to five lessons, outlined below.

*Step 1: Knowledge*

Teach students what plagiarism is. You might do this through a guided exploration or even engage students in an activity where they need to navigate different aspects of the concept, such as plagiarism versus paraphrasing, quoting versus copying, and understanding authorized versus unauthorized use.

*Step 2: Expansion*

As a part of building learners' knowledge about plagiarism, move students to application by exploring real-world examples of plagiarism and its repercussions. We suggest sharing examples that are specific to AI cases, such as the firing of *Sports Illustrated* CEO Ross Levinsohn in December 2023 for posting AI-generated stories from fake writers (Kraft, 2023).

*Step 3: Analysis*

After students have gained a deeper understanding of plagiarism and all the nuances around it, it is important to have them look closely at references: both in-text citations and works cited pages. This is the ideal time to teach students how to cite the use of AI and explain where and when it is appropriate. Major citation systems used in schools, including the Modern Language Association (MLA; 2023; https://style.mla.org/citing-generative-ai/) and the American Psychological Association (APA; 2023; https://apastyle.apa.org/blog/how-to-cite-chatgpt), have guidelines for appropriate citation of AI-generated content.

*Step 4: Synthesis*

During synthesis, have students work with their own writing using AI. As part of this task, ask them to determine when and where to add citations. This is a perfect opportunity to model for students and have them engage in active practice, including working in groups or partnerships. Students may need several opportunities to practice this step.

*Step 5: Evaluation*

As you reach the end of this series of lessons, ask students to engage in evaluation. Guide students to revisit the discussions held on the first day and identify their evolution of knowledge about what *plagiarism* is and why it is an important concept to learn. As a culminating activity, Vosen (2008) proposes that the class can debate topics such as "Should students fail if they plagiarize?" We imagine that you could make AI a part of this debate topic too.

In the coming years, we are likely to see formalized policies for schools and organizations about what is and is not considered acceptable with the use of AI-generated content. That said, even after policies are established, the guidelines are likely to be revised as familiarity with the tools, their capabilities, and the limitations become more apparent. In fact, in early 2023, some school districts—including Baltimore, Los Angeles, and New York City—enacted policies restricting the use of AI; within three months they reversed their stance.

## RESPONSIBLE ANALYSIS OF OUTPUT

As educators, we know it is important to be mindful of what we put in front of students. We review assignments, print and digital texts, and multimedia to make sure that the content is appropriate for our audience and that the materials help us reach a necessary learning intention. While AI may initially appear as superhuman, it is crucial that educators look carefully with a critical eye at the content it generates, just as you would any other new resource. The beauty of AI is that if the original output is not exactly what you intended, you can ask for revisions and changes until you get an end product that matches your intention.

The report *Artificial Intelligence and the Future of Teaching and Learning* by the U.S. Department of Education's Office of Technology (2023) is instructive. The report emphasizes the crucial involvement of a human in the loop, and it stresses that teachers must remain at the helm of all instructional decisions about material used and feedback given. The authors of the report also stress that AI has limitations and that human users must exercise professional judgment when looking at the material AI generates.

In most cases, you will find that there is no need to revise AI output for basic things such as sentence structure and punctuation. Indeed, for a decade or more most of us have used AI communication tools in email systems and as grammar checks. Rather, you should find yourself looking critically at the content provided and the clarity of the output. Does it possess the style and voice you were looking for?

Table 1 contains a list of criteria we have found useful when analyzing the responses we get from AI on teacher-facing and student-facing sites.

## Table 1 • Criteria for Analyzing AI Responses

| Criteria | Questions for Teacher Consideration | Prompts for Revision |
|---|---|---|
| Content | • Is the information accurate?<br>• Are there any misleading or questionable statements?<br>• Does the output match what you are teaching?<br>• Does the information seem appropriate for a specific set of students?<br>• Is the output too much or too little based on the purpose?<br>• Is the information up to date?<br>• Other _____ | • Make the content appropriate for _____.<br>• Change the section about _____.<br>• Revise _____ so that it includes _____.<br>• Where did you get the information included?<br>• Adjust to match the learning standard _____. |
| Clarity | • Is the language clear or are there places it could be clearer?<br>• Is the output organized appropriately?<br>• Does the output match the needs of an audience?<br>• Is there a way output could be more concise?<br>• Other _____ | • Make the content appropriate for _____.<br>• Change the section about _____.<br>• Revise _____ so that it includes _____.<br>• Where did you get the information included? Provide a list of sources.<br>• Adjust to match the learning standard _____. |
| Voice | • Does the output use the same tone as the person using it?<br>• Does the tone match the audience or purpose?<br>• Are there any words or phrases that should be changed or avoided?<br>• Is the language used appropriate for the grade level?<br>• Is the voice too complex or generic?<br>• Other _____ | • Avoid using words like _____ and _____.<br>• Rewrite or regenerate for _____ -grade students.<br>• The purpose of this is to _____. Revise accordingly.<br>• Reword the part about _____ in order to _____. |

## Task Takeover

### Lesson Planning

................................................................................

Using AI to help generate ideas for lessons, learning objectives, and success criteria is one of its great benefits, and it is also the time to use your professional judgment and experience. Let's try another task with AI. Imagine that you want to teach your students a lesson on how they can responsibly use generative AI to revise their own writing.

Step 1: Visit the Eduaide website: https://www.eduaide.ai.

Step 2: Select the Content Generator feature and the Learning Objective and Success Criteria tool.

Step 3: In the Topic or Keyword box, type in "Teach students how to use generative AI responsibly to revise their writing."

Step 4: Analyze the ideas generated using the Criteria for Analyzing AI Responses (Table 1).

- Do the lesson objectives seem appropriate for your students?

- Do the concepts and skills offer a logical learning progression for your class?

- Does the voice and tone sound reasonable for your class?

................................................................................

# CREDIBILITY

At some point, you've probably gone on an unexpected journey on the internet, starting with a search for one thing and finding something else entirely. (Some people call this *going down the rabbit hole*.) While this serendipitous journey is sometimes fun and can be quite informative, users need to consider whether the sources they have encountered on this path are credible. With this in mind, as we have noted, one challenge with the information generated by AI is that it lacks source information. Thus, for educators, it can be quite difficult to teach students about the credibility of the sources they encounter when they are evaluating information generated by AI, because often there are no sources included at all. The use of AI in education brings with it the need for teachers and students to think carefully about the credibility of sources and the information's reliability.

*Credibility* refers to the assurance that information is accurate and that users can trust the sources. As we have noted, content generated by AI presents a unique challenge to source credibility as there is technically no human author. This does not imply that the information provided lacks credibility; rather, it emphasizes the need for human users to critically assess the output and be strategic in how and when they use the generated material. We recognize that AI systems are aggregating content from the internet. For example, when we asked ChatGPT where it obtained the sources for one of our inquiries, the system responded, "My knowledge is derived from the diverse range of sources available on the internet up to my last update in January 2022" (OpenAI, 2023). That's not actually very helpful.

A parallel can be drawn with a situation from the early 2000s: the advent of Wikipedia, a site hailed as the first complete online encyclopedia—a seemingly ideal resource for learning about a wide variety of topics in a short period of time. However, because it is a platform that relies on volunteers and users to contribute information, users soon recognized instances of inaccuracies and bias. While Wikipedia remains among the top ten most visited websites even today, users have learned to approach its information critically, acknowledging its limitations and using it accordingly. Interacting with AI-generated content requires a similar approach.

Analyzing sources for credibility is not a skill unique to Wikipedia and AI. In the age of the internet, social media, and rapid technological dissemination of information, the prevalence of misinformation is huge. Human users must develop the ability to evaluate and question information they encounter across platforms critically. Below are key questions for you and your students to consider when assessing the reliability of information, especially AI-generated information.

- Does the information presented need verification?
- Should additional sources be cross-referenced?
- Is there any inherent bias or one-sidedness in the information?
- Are there alternative perspectives that should be considered?
- Has the information on this topic been updated recently? (Most of the AI systems that we use are updated annually and do not have the most updated information available.)

---

## Ask a Bot

AI itself has the capability to teach users about its credibility, reliability, and even its limitations. Here's a simple way to take some time to engage with an OpenAI site in a conversation that is centered around credibility.

Step 1: Sign in to your favorite OpenAI chatbot.

Step 2: Ask the chatbot guiding questions about its credibility.

- Where do you get your information?
- What sources do you draw from?
- Where do you get your data?
- How do I cross-check the information AI shares?
- Are artificial intelligence sites credible?
- What should users know about the information AI shares?
- How up to date is the content provided through AI?

---

Step 3: Reflect on the experience and consider what you might need to teach students about AI credibility.

- Would you trust this information based on the results shared?
- Would you want to seek any clarification on the information presented?
- Would you change your original request for information based on the AI results?

Effectively learning how to prompt AI and becoming a critical consumer of generated content is a fundamental responsibility for all users. Although this may take time and practice, it is important to recognize the importance of both prompting and responsible use when it comes to effective, but most importantly, ethical use of the tools. In fact, these skills are so important that they are already becoming an important set of skills supported and taught in higher education. Many institutions are now offering dedicated courses on the topic, such as Western Michigan's "AI: Prompt and Response." Some universities have brought together faculty from various departments to lead groups focused on the research, education, and practice behind AI, like HAI (Human-Centered Artificial Intelligence) at Stanford University. Most universities have started implementing guidelines for student use of generative AI on assignments and assessments such as the "Guidelines for Use of Generative Artificial Intelligence in Assessment" at San Diego State University (shared in Figure 6 below). We have no doubt

### Figure 6 • Guidelines for Use of Generative Artificial Intelligence (gAI) in Assessments and Deliverables at SDSU

Principles of use for generative AI (gAI), including systems such as ChatGPT, Bard, and Bing, which can produce content in response to natural language queries, is becoming increasingly prevalent. Students need to understand the principles guiding gAI use in assessments and deliverables. Proficiency, verification, and documentation are key principles to keep in mind:

A. Proficiency: Proficiency is more than just memorizing facts. It involves building flexible knowledge structures to solve problems and evaluate potential solutions. Use gAI effectively, students should have a firm grasp on the subject matter.

B. Verification: Students must take full responsibility for gAI-generated materials, ensuring they are accurate and factually sound. Generative AI can produce incorrect or misleading information, making verification crucial.

C. Documentation: Proper documentation is essential for all non-original ideas and sources, as gAI may create fictional references, also known as "hallucinations." When documentation is required, students must follow standard practices for cit-ing sources.

Classification levels of allowed use of gAI in Assessments and Deliverables: The following classification levels determine the permitted use of gAI in-course assessments and deliverables:

- AI-1: Disallowed
- AI-2: Restricted
- AI-3: Documented
- AI-4: Unrestricted

Source: San Diego State University, 2024.

that K–12 schools, districts, and states will follow suit, in fact many already have, and hope this chapter and those that follow will help build your skillset and understanding for all there is to come.

## Check for Understanding

Consider the following AI-generated discussion questions. If you are reading alone, feel free to write responses. Alternatively, if you are able, engage in meaningful dialogue with colleagues. Use all you have learned in this chapter to discuss prompt writing, the ethics of AI, and the task of teaching students about plagiarism. (See Appendix for answers to all Check for Understanding questions.)

Discussion Question #1: What are your concerns about integrating AI into education, particularly in terms of ethical use and avoiding plagiarism? How do you think educators can address these concerns effectively?

Discussion Question #2: Considering the guidelines provided for crafting strong prompts for AI, how important do you think it is for educators to master the skill of communicating with AI systems? What potential challenges do you foresee in prompt writing for AI, and how could these be mitigated?

Discussion Question #3: How can educators effectively teach students about plagiarism in the context of AI-generated content? What strategies or activities could you employ to ensure students understand the ethical use of AI-generated material and the importance of proper citation and attribution?

## CONCLUSION

Writing a good prompt is key to getting useful information from AI systems. However, this process is not just a one-shot deal. If you review the response and it's not what you expected, needed, or wanted, then you can provide additional prompts to get closer to the information you want. We hope that you have practiced creating prompts using the aspects outlined in this chapter. And we hope that you were able to evaluate the quality and credibility of the information that was provided. In doing so, you're using critical thinking skills, and your students will develop those skills as well. Along the way, you'll need to teach students about plagiarism and how to cite their sources. While this task can be challenging when it comes to evaluating the sources for material generated by AI, we hope the discussions in this chapter will help you make a start.

# Part 2

# Why & How to Use AI

# Educator Function #1

## Managing Content

> **EDUCATOR FUNCTION**
>
> - Generate, organize, revise, and consolidate curriculum or content based on students' learning needs.

Every job has essential functions: tasks and responsibilities necessary to fulfill the role. For educators, our responsibility is to supervise, instruct, and support students in achieving certain learning benchmarks. This involves lesson planning around targeted skills, managing classroom behavior and student productivity, keeping students continuously engaged in learning, and providing regular supportive feedback. Almost every aspect of the teacher's job demands flexibility and takes time for planning and preparation: time to create, re-create, adjust, organize, and process.

A major role that educators have focuses on the *what* and *how* of school: what students need to learn and how they will learn it. Our state standards provide an overview or set of outcomes in terms of what students need to know and be able to do for each year of school in each subject. Teachers also have access to instructional materials that are designed to help them know how to provide students' access to the standards. Yet regardless of what standards and materials are provided, teachers must still spend time planning and preparing content that they deliver. AI is here to help make all of this more manageable.

## ✏️ Stop and Jot
### Reflecting on Job Function

Take some time to reflect on job functions specific to your position. Keep these reflections in mind as the chapters and Educator Functions in this playbook explore how AI can assist you. These reflections will guide you in determining where you might want to start.

What parts of your job take the most time?

_____

_____

Where do you wish you were more efficient?

_____

_____

What required tasks do you think could be automated?

_____

_____

If you had the time, what is one thing you would spend more time doing in your classroom?

_____

_____

Many educators already rely on some technology-based tools to assist them in performing tasks such as keeping track of grades and taking attendance. Whether teachers are utilizing digital curriculum resources, adaptive assessment platforms with intervention plans, interactive whiteboards, tablets, or one of many internet sites, the use of technology as a tool to help educators function is not a new concept. AI, like many other tech-based teaching tools, offers the opportunity to help educators with their growing list of job responsibilities. One opportunity focuses on managing the content that students will learn.

Tammy Jessop is a middle school science teacher. After learning about a teacher-facing AI site for the first time, she decided to try using it to assess one student's essay against a rubric. Ms. Jessop had used for the same assignment for several years. To begin, she uploaded the student essay and the rubric. Then she asked the AI tool to analyze the students' work against the criteria. Within seconds, she had a completed rubric for the student essay, but she was disappointed to see that the results were nowhere near what she would have generated on her own. The comments were generic such as "unclear claim" and "contains no explanation." However, instead of giving up on the AI tool, she decided to look critically at the rubric it had produced, and she realized that some parts of her own rubric lacked clarity and needed more specific criteria. She spent time making revisions, and in the end she not only had a stronger rubric for the assignment but also was confident that, moving forward, she would be able to take advantage of an AI tool that would help her accurately assess student work.

# ARTIFICIAL INTELLIGENCE–ASSISTED TEACHER FUNCTIONS

AI holds incredible potential, but navigating the range of applications and understanding how the tools can enhance daily tasks can be overwhelming. You are likely to discover, as we have, that the more often you engage with AI in daily classroom functions, the more ways you will come to find it useful. By exploring broader categories of AI-assisted functionalities for teachers, you will gain your own insights into how helpful this resource can and will be to the field of education. In this Educator Function, we focus on the content. We have organized the ways in which AI can assist with content into four areas: content generation, content organization, content revision, and content consolidation.

## Self-Assessment

*Use the scale to assess your use of AI to engage in common teacher functions when it comes to curriculum. What areas do you want to strengthen?*

| Curriculum Innovations | |
|---|---|
| Content Generation<br><br>• Asking AI systems to produce content and instructional materials that you can use with students | |
| Content Organization<br><br>• Asking AI systems to organize the existing content into new formats or structures | |
| Content Revision<br><br>• Asking AI systems to revise existing content based on student needs, priorities for learning, or levels of background knowledge | |
| Content Consolidation<br><br>• Asking AI systems to identify essential features for learning and produce a flow that meets certain time constraints | |

# CONTENT GENERATION

When you use AI appropriately to generate content, it can serve as your thought partner and help you develop your ideas. For example, if you are considering how to teach a new standard, if you would like to rethink something you have taught before, if you find yourself searching for additional materials, or if you have students needing more practice with a specific skill, you can now start with AI. When you use specific prompts to describe what you are looking for, AI can offer creative and innovative content—with responses that come from a vast body of data and a diverse set of sources—in a fraction of the time it might take a human user to generate similar material.

Examples of tasks AI can handle to produce useful content include the following:

- Creating math problems and tasks
- Crafting the morning message
- Developing games for practice of concepts
- Writing stories for social emotional learning
- Identifying possible themes in stories
- Creating a choice board for students to complete tasks

With content generation it is important to remember that looking carefully at output and being mindful of how it fits instructional needs is essential. As noted in Chapter 2, users have the responsibility to carefully examine the content generated by AI and make revisions and changes as needed. We encourage educators to see AI as a great place to start generating content, a tool to help speed up pace or give a little boost, but not lose sight of the importance in providing students with reliable, aligned, and evidence-based materials to support them in learning, practice and understanding.

## Try It Out!

### Generate Content

Step 1: Consider the questions below to identify a topic you would like to generate content for.

- What is a new topic, concept, or skill you will be teaching?
- What is a lesson you have taught before that you would like to change or modify?
- When planning _____, what would you like to find more of?
- Is there something you are currently teaching, or a resource you are using, that could be strengthened?
- Which topic or standard prompts you to search for additional teaching materials?

Step 2: Visit your favorite chatbot on an OpenAI site.

Step 3: Complete and enter one of the prompts below:

- Prompt Option 1: *Create a [lesson/set of problems/example of] for _____ -grade students. Focus on _____ and _____, allowing students to practice _____.*

- Prompt Option 2: *I am a _____ teacher looking for ideas on how to teach _____. Give me _____ ideas that include _____ and _____.*

- Prompt Option 3: [Create your own prompt using an answer or thought from the questions in Step 1.]

Step 4: Review and reprompt if necessary.

We would also like to share several prompt recommendations that can increase the value of the material that AI produces for you. As you ask AI to generate content, keep in mind the prompting suggestions provided in Part 1, and consider taking these additional steps.

- Specify the desired length or number of problems you want generated. Additionally, consider indicating specific timeframes (e.g., 10 minutes, one week, a month).

- Include the grade level or age of learners in your prompt. If applicable, you can also copy and paste a specific standard or success criteria to address.

- Work with AI to adjust the length of output using simple cues like *make longer* or *make shorter* until you get desired results.

## Classroom Connection

### Students Using AI to Generate Ideas

Idea generation plays a crucial role in every writing assignment, whether the student is selecting a topic to write about or ideas for specific vocabulary to include. As students master effective prompting techniques, knowing what to ask and how to ask it, they can leverage AI tools as thought partners. With modeling, educators can teach students how to use AI effectively when generating ideas for a written assignment. Here are some prompts and questions you might use with students when helping them use AI assistance during this part of the writing process.

- *Help me think about ideas for a personal narrative.*

- *What vocabulary should be included when writing about _____?*

- *What are potential counterarguments to my claim?*

- *What are opposing viewpoints about _____?*

- *What are misconceptions I should address when writing about _____?*

## CONTENT ORGANIZATION

Educators are well versed in organization; it is an essential component of the job. Organizing your classroom routines involves making decisions about instruction; it also requires arranging, categorizing, and sorting student work. While some curriculum resources provide suggested structures for a lesson or unit, teachers often find themselves rethinking the way things unfold in the classroom because of time constraints, student needs, background knowledge, and personal preferences and priorities. With the appropriate prompting, AI will provide innovative ideas for content organization; in fact, AI can effectively reorganize materials if you have a specific a focus in mind. Additionally, AI will assist you with the second major organizational job function, which is sorting, arranging, and categorizing student work.

Examples of AI's ability to help you organize content include but are not limited to the following:

- Developing learning progressions based on analysis of the standards

- Creating a list of steps for student practice

- Arranging a list of lessons in a certain order

- Sorting digital exit tickets to identify strengths and needs

- Forming student groups based on common needs

## Ask a Bot

Consider a topic that you plan to teach, whether it be linear equations or the solar system or literary devices. Ask an OpenAI site to order the content in a logical way for teaching a specific grade level. As an example, we asked about the best order for teaching third-grade students about fractions. ChatGPT offered this suggestion:

> Begin by introducing parts of a whole and unit fractions, progress to comparing and creating equivalent fractions, then move on to addition, subtraction, multiplication, and division of fractions, gradually incorporating mixed numbers and real-world word problems to reinforce understanding. Throughout, use visual aids and hands-on activities to enhance comprehension and engage students in the learning process. (OpenAI, 2023)

What topic did you ask about?

What information was useful for you?

## CONTENT REVISION

Revision takes time—one commodity that educators always feel is in short supply. Yet, because of time constraints, we may ultimately decide to teach a lesson in the same way that was not effective in the past or give the exact same assignment we have done before even though we know it could be improved. With AI, revisions are easier to navigate. AI tools have the capability to help us adapt student assignments so they take on a new focus. In this way, we can also fine-tune lessons to fit new time limitations or address a new audience.

Examples of revising content include the following:

- Changing the topic of a mentor text
- Making an existing lesson easier or more complex
- Revising a study guide for a new focus
- Creating a practice test
- Revising a rubric with additions or substitutions

## Classroom Connection

### Students Using AI for Revision

Teaching students to effectively revise their own work is a skill taught across K–12 classrooms, especially in the context of written assignments. This skill is both an important part of work production and the learning process. Rather than solely relying on AI to revise work for them, it is important to guide students in approaching the use of AI for revision from a different angle. Teach students ways they can engage with AI to get revision suggestions, all while modeling the importance of being specific in what one is revising for—something important with or without the use of technology.

We suggest starting by modeling the output difference between two prompts such as, *What suggestions do you have for revisions?* and *I want my readers to know important this historical event was to American History. What suggestions do you have for how I can revise the voice or word choice in my writing to help me do this?* As students compare revision suggestions, they will see the importance of having a clear vision for revision and you will be teaching how to ask AI for support in a way that doesn't yield automatic changes. You might even consider having students draft possible prompts from less specific to more specific before even using the tools. The art of learning to craft these prompts will not only be a way to bring AI into the classroom but will help students learn the power of and possibility in true, thoughtful revision.

## CONTENT CONSOLIDATION

Another common challenge for educators is the need to consolidate content to fit time constraints created by unexpected events, such as student assemblies or snow days. Sometimes it seems that there will never be time to do it all. Although there are often opportunities to blend concepts and create lessons or units that address multiple standards or integrate multiple subject areas, this strategic planning can be time-consuming. AI can play a valuable role in making this type of planning more efficient. Functioning much like a colleague or coplanner (though one that works at a much quicker speed), AI can serve as a starting point for merging ideas. Specifically, it can quickly synthesize multiple texts—such as success criteria, directions, or teaching points—into a cohesive plan. Additionally, it can offer you guidance when you must navigate multiple subjects, such as writing, social studies, and reading, within a limited time frame.

Examples of consolidating content include the following:

- Merging two lesson plans together
- Combining multiple student samples into one
- Integrating different types of problems into one practice or assessment set
- Creating a learning experience that combines science and reading

### Try It Out!

#### Consolidate Content

Step 1: Think of two topics, lessons, or standards you need to cover.

#1 _____

#2 _____

Step 2: Using this list, or an idea of your own, decide on what output you would like AI to provide.

- Learning intention
- Success criteria
- Teaching point
- Lesson plan
- Student activity
- Exemplar
- Assessment tool

Step 3: Visit your favorite chatbot on an OpenAI site.

Step 4: Complete and enter one of the prompts below.

- Prompt Option 1: *Create a _____ for _____ grade that combines _____ and _____.*
- Prompt Option 2: *I am looking for an idea on how to consolidate _____ and _____ into _____ days/weeks. Create a _____ for _____ grade that fits these guidelines.*
- Prompt Option 3: [Create your own using answers from Step 1 and Step 2.]

Step 4: Review and reprompt if necessary. Some additional prompt recommendations for combining content include these:

- If you do not want something included, prompt AI accordingly, using phrases like *Do not include _____*, or *Avoid using _____ and _____*.
- If you have an idea for what you want the output to look like (e.g., a paragraph, a chart, a list of assignments, or a description of a sequence of lessons), include those details in the prompt.

Although AI can support many teaching functions, the user's proficiency with AI and AI tools is a critical factor. In this way, the use of AI is not unlike the use of other technological tools available to educators. For instance, two users who have access to the same interactive whiteboard could easily have different experiences. The user who is more experienced with its functions and has explored its capabilities is likely to benefit more from having access to the technology in the classroom. Investing time to learn about AI is an integral aspect of the process. It's not just about learning what it is and how to use it; it's also about taking the time to get to know how it can work for you and your specific job functions.

Having a clear objective in mind before engaging with AI tools for content creation is essential. The U.S. Department of Education's Office of Technology (2023) compares using technology-enhanced education to riding an electric bike: The effectiveness of AI tools hinges on the user's understanding of their capabilities and vision for desired output. Unless the user has a clear direction or purpose, the outcomes may not align with the expectations.

An electric bike requires a human user who can steer it in the right direction and at a suitable pace given the terrain. Similarly, if you approach an AI task without some specificity in your request, the results will reflect that. The left column in Table 2 includes examples of AI requests that lack specificity and could use more direction. The right column provides robust prompts that focus more precisely on what the human user has in mind; these prompts increase the likelihood that the content generated will be useful.

## Table 2 • Revising Prompts for Common Teacher Tasks

| Instead of This | Try This |
|---|---|
| Unpack this learning standard. | What are three helpful tips when teaching students about _____? |
| | What academic vocabulary should students know when learning about _____? |
| | What common mistakes do students make when learning about _____? |
| | What are misconceptions to address when teaching _____? |
| Write a lesson plan for _____. | What should students do to practice _____? |
| | Provide a step-by-step process for teaching _____. |
| | What is a plan for teaching _____ to a group of students who have already done _____? |
| | Help me think through how to explain the purpose of learning about _____ to students. |
| | What is a student-friendly learning objective for _____? |
| | What are sentence stems to use as student scaffolds when teaching about _____? |

*(Continued)*

(Continued)

| Instead of This | Try This |
|---|---|
| Write a multiple-choice assessment. | What are good multiple-choice questions to ask students who need to practice _____ ? |
| | Create assessment questions with _____ choices that have students practice _____ ; include answers. |
| | Create an assessment that will provide data about _____ . |
| Give an example of _____ . | Write an example of _____ that includes _____ and _____ . |
| | What will students need to see when working on _____ ? |
| | Can you give a _____ word example and nonexample to show _____ -grade students? |

## Task-Takeover

### Analyzing Standards

For this takeover, we will be trying to get to know a standard in preparation of an upcoming second-grade social studies lesson.

Step 1: Visit ChatGPT or your favorite AI model and open a new chat.

Step 2: In the chatbox, enter CCSS standard RI2.3: *Describe the connection between a series of historical events, scientific ideas or concepts, or steps in technical procedures in a text.*

Step 3: Add this prompt: *Please help my colleagues and me unpack this learning standard.*

Step 4: Review the generated response before entering the next request. Now we'll try a different approach.

Step 5: Reenter the same standard, CCSS RI2.3: *Describe the connection between a series of historical events, scientific ideas or concepts, or steps in technical procedures in a text.* Then add one of these requests:

- What are three helpful tips when teaching students about this standard?
- What academic vocabulary should students know when learning about this academic standard?

Step 6: Review the generated response and note the ways that the different prompts provide you with different information.

Getting to know a standard for the first time or revisiting a familiar standard is an important exercise for developing units of instruction. However, there are many dimensions for calibrating a standard to instruction that go well beyond understanding its meaning. For instance, you may consider the nouns and noun phrases (concepts) and verbs or verb phrases (skills) that students need to know (Fisher et al., 2024). AI can help you quickly identify these concepts and skills within the standard and even start to create learning progressions. Carefully crafted prompts, like those shared here, allow teachers to generate planning material that is useful and time-saving.

## Check for Understanding

We created a handful of AI-generated scenarios related to the content in this Educator Function using features available on multiple teacher-facing AI sites. Take some time to apply what you have learned about how AI can assist in content creation for each situation presented. (See Appendix for answers to all Check for Understanding questions.)

Scenario 1: As a middle school science teacher, you are looking to use AI to help you generate content for a new unit you will be teaching next month. Specifically, you would like help on engaging experiments. How could you use AI to generate creative and innovative ideas for science labs in this unit? What are all the ways you can use AI tools to help? What types of content can it generate to help with the overall teaching experience?

Scenario 2: You are a third-grade teacher tasked with integrating content areas with literacy. You decide to integrate social studies with speaking and listening into a cohesive learning experience for students. How would you leverage AI to consolidate content and create a comprehensive lesson that incorporates concepts from both subjects?

Scenario 3: You are an English teacher who has thirteen instructional days before an upcoming break. You are teaching an argument-writing unit and, according to the curriculum resource being used, you have nineteen sessions to teach. How could you use AI to help you arrange this unit in a way that allows you to fit it in before the break? What details will be important to include when seeking assistance from AI?

## CONCLUSION

Thinking about all the ways AI can assist with daily functions doesn't end here. This chapter has provided you with ways to generate, organize, revise, and consolidate the curriculum and content that your students need to learn using AI tools to make your professional life a bit easier. Throughout the rest of this playbook, we will take a deeper look into more ways that AI can and will change the landscape of teacher planning, instruction, and assessment in positive ways. We hope that the information in this Educator Function is already saving you time!

# Educator Function #2

## Fostering Student Engagement

**EDUCATOR FUNCTION CHALLENGE**

- Use AI to increase relevance for students and invite students to engage in the various tasks you create.

With our content ready, our next task is to engage students in meaningful learning. We want students to dive into tasks, maintain their focus, push aside distractions, and learn. Engagement is an essential part of learning. The more engaged learners are, the more they will gain from a given lesson. And when students find the content and lesson relevant, they are more likely to engage.

Capturing the attention of learners—which entails getting them involved in a lesson cognitively, behaviorally, and emotionally—is no small feat. With each new class, educators are charged with the task of finding ways to capture students' attention. We create tasks students will find interesting, plan connections that relate to students' interests, and teach students strategies they can independently employ to make content more accessible and interesting.

This can all be extremely challenging for teachers. What engages one learner might not be the same for another. And, quite frankly, we have not had time to customize all our lessons to ensure that students find the content relevant. But AI can help. As we will see in this chapter, there are ways to address the role of background knowledge, choice, gamified learning, and relevance with AI. And we can directly teach students about engagement and use tools to invite students into learning. While these systems cannot replace the relationship between the student and the teacher, which we recognize is a major reason that students choose to engage, AI can make it easier for educators to accomplish other things so that they have more time to develop strong relationships with their students.

**Stop and Jot**

Take a few minutes to think about specific students and their interests. Later in this chapter, you can develop these topics further and write prompts for AI to use with your students in mind.

| | Facts About Student | Interests of Student |
|---|---|---|
| Student: | | |
| Student: | | |
| Student: | | |
| Student: | | |

# FOSTERING BACKGROUND KNOWLEDGE

Our students' background knowledge significantly impacts their overall understanding and comprehension of the content, tasks, and texts we assign. When we activate our students' background knowledge, we pique their interest and invite them to actively engage in their learning.

We can teach students to be active learners by giving them strategies for building background knowledge before beginning a new unit or just before studying a new topic. Of course, a quick Google search could build some background knowledge, but with AI tools we can do so much more. For instance, there are student-facing sites that are designed to give students the opportunity to engage with a chatbot for a back-and-forth conversation using a teacher-created prompt. This approach sparks students' interest and gets them thinking about a topic. On many platforms, teachers can see student conversations and use student dialogic engagement with AI as a preassessment for future teaching.

For example, a team of physical education and health teachers are getting ready to start a unit on nutrition. The teachers understand that engaging the class from the start is important. They decide that on the first day, in place of using the K–W–L chart (the class-generated graphic organizer where students share what they know and want to know about the topic and later add what they've learned), they will spark engagement by modeling a preplanned conversation using AI.

Using the Study Buddy tool from Socrat.ai, which evaluates the student's current understanding and helps guide their learning further, the teachers assign students to have a guided conversation with a bot. They start with the idea of nutrients and the system goes back and forth with questions, providing additional information when students are confused.

By entering a little bit of information in advance (see Figure 7), sites like socrat.ai can help teachers create learning experiences that require students' participation and get them thinking about a topic without a typical teacher lecture or "raise your hand and tell me know what you know" experience.

**Figure 7** • Socrat.ai Study Buddy Assignment Creator

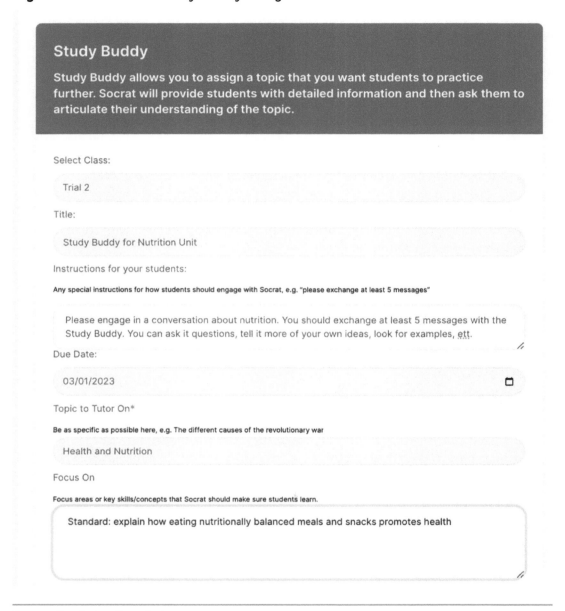

Source: Created on Socrat.ai.

## Try It Out!

### Creating a Study Buddy Assignment for Student Engagement

Step 1: Log into your teacher dashboard on Socrat.ai.

Step 2: Get started by entering the information needed in "Create Class."

Step 3: Move onto "Create Assignment" and Select Assignment: Study Buddy.

Step 4: Follow prompts from there to create your own Study Buddy assignment.

Step 5: Try it out! Go to View Assignments and Chat to practice the conversations your students will be engaging in once you assign them to do so.

Prompt Recommendations

- Try out your prompt after creating it, as if you were a student. Think about the types of questions it is asking and make revisions accordingly.

- Be specific when telling it what you want students to talk about.

- Tell the chatbot the number of questions and responses you want students to engage in.

## ARTIFICIAL INTELLIGENCE FOR RELEVANCE

The way AI chatbots can help educators change content, create new material, and produce relevant examples is a game changer for education. We can now easily take generic fifth-grade examples from the past and change them to include specific student names, interests, and personal experiences. We can create examples that are a compilation of students' own words. We can efficiently create experiences that captivate and engross each individual in our classroom. We can use technology to help us create learning experiences that deeply engage each learner. The best part is that this only takes minutes, at most, to accomplish.

When we make teaching relevant to students, we engage them in learning by helping them make meaningful connections. The continuum below shows different layers of relevance, the ultimate being personal identification.

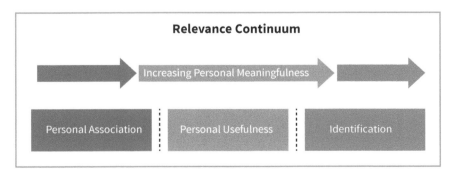

The most current framework of relevance suggests that identification—including topics specific to an individual's identity (facts and interests about specific students)—has significant motivational benefits (Priniski et al., 2018). Individual interest draws in an audience and gives good reasons for learners to stay engaged in the lesson that follows. Let's see what this might actually look like in a classroom.

Calvin and Jake, who are in fifth grade, show little interest in learning about many new topics. Calvin would rather be reading or rereading any Rick Riordan book than "doing school," and Jake only seems to want to talk about riding ATVs with his cousins on weekends. Now their class is starting a science unit on chemical reactions, and their teacher Stasja Drecun knows that if she doesn't engage these two (and others like them) from the start, it will be a tough sell.

Using AI, Ms. Drecun does a basic search on a chatbot, requesting ideas for chemical reaction examples for Olympians or ATV lovers. She also tries the *Make it Relevant* feature on MagicSchool.ai (see Figure 8). Within seconds, the teacher has ideas for a dynamic start to this unit that will get students motivated right off the bat.

**Figure 8** • MagicSchool "Make it Relevant!" Feature

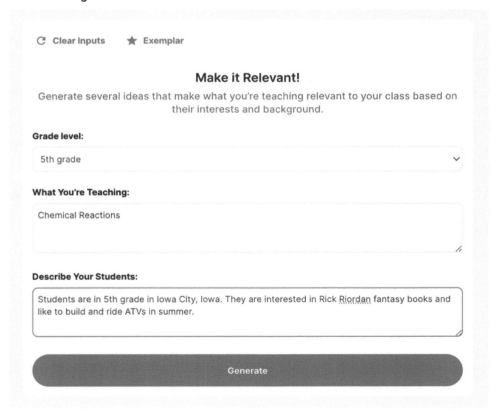

(Continued)

### Idea 1: The Magical Ingredients

Introduce the concept of chemical reactions by drawing parallels to the magical ingredients found in Rick Riordan's fantasy books. Begin by explaining that just like the characters in the books, scientists also work with different ingredients to create amazing reactions.

Activity: Create a "Magical Potion" Experiment

1. Divide the class into small groups and provide each group with a set of different household materials (e.g. baking soda, vinegar, lemon juice, salt, etc.).
2. Ask the students to predict what will happen when they mix two ingredients together.
3. Have them mix the ingredients and observe the reactions. Encourage them to think about the changes they observe, such as bubbles, fizzing, or color changes.
4. Discuss with the whole class how the reactions were similar to or different from what they expected. Relate these observations to the concept of chemical reactions.

### Idea 2: ATV Fuel Adventure

Relate the concept of chemical reactions to the students' love for riding ATVs in the summer. Connect the importance of fueling ATVs with the idea that chemical reactions are used to power various vehicles.

Activity: Designing the Perfect ATV Fuel

1. Discuss with the students the importance of fuel for operating ATVs efficiently.
2. Explain that fuel is created through a specific chemical reaction called combustion, which happens inside the ATV's engine.
3. Divide the class into small groups and provide them with information about different fuel sources, such as gasoline, ethanol, or biodiesel.
4. Ask each group to research and design their own "perfect" fuel for an ATV, considering factors like efficiency, environmental impact, and safety.
5. Allow the groups to present their findings and explain the chemical reactions involved in their fuel choices.

Source: Created on MagicSchool.ai.

## Task Take Over

### Make It Relevant!

Step 1: Sign in to www.magicschool.ai.

Step 2: Select the Magic Tool "Make it Relevant!"

Step 3: Fill in the form with the necessary information, including subject and grade level.

Step 4: Where prompted, use the facts about students and topics of interest to describe your students.

Step 5: Generate and review for content and clarity.

Step 6: Engage learners.

Tapping into individual interests to increase relevance is not the only way teachers can use AI technology to increase engagement in K–12 classrooms. There are other practical ways AI can help. Using informed prompting and knowledge of resources, teachers can create personalized learning experiences, gamify instruction, and make content appropriate for specific audiences to increase overall student engagement. The best part is that with AI, we don't have to start from scratch. We now have the capability to take assignments and lessons that already exist and use them to create experiences that are more personalized to our students and to the cultural and experiential assets they bring to the classroom.

## Self-Assessment

Consider aspects of relevance and how you can make learning relevant for students. What areas do you want to strengthen? How might AI help?

| Aspects of Relevance (Fisher et al., 2023) | |
|---|---|
| There is a consideration of the relevancy connection for the lesson prior to instruction. | |
| Relevancy statements are closely connected to students and not to a distant goal. | |
| Relevancy statements allow students to make a personal association (a connection to an object or memory). | |
| Relevancy statements promote the belief that a task or text will help students reach a personal goal. | |
| Relevancy is provided so students recognize that the task or text is aligned with their identify and their ability to impact others. | |
| Relevancy statements are directly shared with students. | |

## Ask a Bot

Take a few minutes to learn more about why student engagement is essential and how we can support student engagement in the classroom.

1. Sign in to your favorite chatbot.

2. Ask the chatbot guiding questions about student engagement.

   • How would you describe student engagement?

   • What are ways to engage grade _____ students in _____?

   • How can teachers of _____ engage students in learning?

   • What suggestions do you have for engaging students who _____?

3. Continue the conversation with the chatbot, using the add-on prompts below.

- *Say more . . .*

- *Can you give me an example?*

- *Please explain . . .*

- *What would this mean for someone who teaches _____?*

- *I have a student who _____. What would this mean for them?*

4. Reflect

- Ahhhhh. I already do this _____.

- AH HA! This is a new idea _____.

- HMMMMM. I'm not so sure about _____.

## INCREASING CHOICE TO INCREASE ENGAGEMENT

Choice is another powerful strategy for increasing engagement and motivation for students' learning pathways. Teachers must engage in both planning and forethought to find effective ways to provide choice while retaining control of the skills and concepts students are learning as well as the materials they use to do so.

Some educators use a choice board—a menu of targeted learning tasks—to create a selection of activities to provide learners with control over the pace and path of their learning. These menus provide students with options for activities to engage in, questions to answer, texts to read, and problems to solve. The beauty is that they can be used flexibly at different times during the day (e.g., independent work time, intervention blocks, or morning work). This is another area where AI can save teachers some of the time they would typically spend searching for choice boards that already exist through a Google search or a third-party purchase; the use of AI also allows teachers to ensure that the choice boards are personal.

In one district we work in, there has been a push for teachers in middle school and high school to create choice boards specific to data-driven student needs. Though this generally is a great idea, the teachers have struggled with the time it takes to look at the data and create the tool itself. They have spent time looking at data during department meetings, so they know what students need to work on, but until now, they have lacked the time to create a variety of learning tasks. Today, however, education-specific AI sites give a Choice Board option. After following the sites' guided prompts, teachers can generate a customized Choice Board within minutes.

Source: Created on Eduaide.ai.

## Try It Out!

### Create a Student Choice Board

Step 1: Sign into either teacher-facing AI platform, Eduaide.ai or MagicSchool.ai.

Step 2: Submit necessary information about the subject and grade level.

Step 3: Select "Choice Board Assignments."

Step 4: Develop a prompt that provides details about the content you want to be included in the choice board generated. Here is an example:

> *Students are in a US government course. This choice board should prompt them to engage in lessons and activities that help them better understand the United States government across history. All assignments should allow students to work independently and will be additional practice.*

Step 5: Generate a choice board.

Step 6: Analyze the output and make any needed changes by editing or adjusting the prompt.

## Prompt Recommendations

- Be as specific as possible with the skills students should be practicing.

- Tell the chatbot how you want students to practice (i.e., independently or in groups).

- Provide a time frame for how long choice options should take.

- Request that it provide materials needed for each choice.

- Name the materials you have on hand for students to use.

# GAMIFY LEARNING

Most people like games; the competitive nature of gaming, the motivation to win, and the enjoyment associated with the idea of a game usually draw participants. Psychological research suggests that since humans like challenges and have a deep desire to reach a finish line, games zero in on this natural longing and act as motivation for the task (or learning) at hand. This approach, of course, is not unique to education. For instance, Nike has an app that gets people working out by offering badges athletes can earn by completing certain fitness challenges. Pokémon has retained the interest of kids and adults by creating an app-based game called Pokémon Go that, at its peak, had more than 177 million active users (Liang, 2023).

Gaming increases active participation and engagement. In education, whether it be a *Jeopardy!*–style test review or a rousing game of Headbands to practice science vocabulary, teachers often use games to make learning enjoyable and memorable; this approach often motivates students to do work that might otherwise seem boring and mundane. Games can mask the heavy lifting or not-so-fun feel that sometimes comes with learning.

AI can help gamify what might feel like dry lessons or content that a teacher has to get to but that students might not be particularly interested in doing. One simple way to gamify material is to ask your favorite chatbot for ideas. Here are a few examples of prompts that can be quite effective.

*Give me ideas for games that help students practice multiplication. What are some games I can use in my music class to teach about rhythm?*

These prompts should generate multiple ideas, and the results will probably even remind you of things you've done in the past that would apply to the content you're wanting learners to practice.

You can also use AI to turn existing lessons into a game. For example, Marco Ramirez knew that vocabulary was an area of need for his seventh-grade English class. He recognized that rote practice of terms was not the answer, so he decided to gamify the material. He decided to use Rasinski and Cheesman-Smith's word ladder structure (2020) that requires students read clues for each rung of the ladder and change or rearrange letters to create words until they reach the top. In doing so, students analyze grapheme–phoneme relationships, broadening their vocabulary, and building spelling skills. Mr. Ramirez entered this prompt into ChatGPT:

*Make a Word Ladder game with _____ words going from _____ to _____. Please include clues about the number of letters changed, added, or subtracted, and give a vocabulary clue about each new word.*

Here is the AI-generated content he modified for his word ladder vocabulary game, which his class played in partnerships the next day:

**ChatGPT**

Of course! Here is the revised 10-word word ladder from "stingray" to "pickle" with simpler terms:

1. stingray (Marine animal with a venomous stinger)
2. stringy (Resembling thin threads)
   * Change two letters to describe a texture.
3. strong (Having great power or influence)
   * Change two letters to suggest power or robustness.
4. song (Musical composition with lyrics)
   * Remove one letter to indicate a piece of music.
5. sign (Indication or gesture)
   * Change one letter to suggest a symbol or indicator.
6. sing (Produce musical sounds with the voice)
   * Remove one letter to denote vocalization.
7. sin (Morally or ethically wrong act)
   * Remove one letter to denote wrongdoing.
8. bin (Container for storage)
   * Change one letter to indicate a receptacle.
9. bike (Two-wheeled vehicle)
   * Change one letter to suggest a mode of transportation.
10. pickle (Vegetable preserved in brine or vinegar)
    * Change one letter to suggest a preserved food item.

 ↓

Source: Created on ChatGPT.com.

Initially the result wasn't perfect, so Mr. Ramirez made revisions to the clues to more accurately reflect the number of letters to be altered, added, or deleted. However, the initial results gave him a great start on creating the word game for his students.

## Try It Out!

### Making a Word Ladder Game to Gamify Vocabulary Practice

Step 1: Sign into a chatbot site.

Step 2: Customize this prompt for your class. You can use words that personalize the experience, like *pickle* (this teacher's favorite snack) and *stingray* (the school mascot);

words related to something specific being studied in class; or just a couple of words that students might find fun.

> Prompt: *Make a Word Ladder game with _____ words going from _____ to _____. Include clues about the number of letters changed, added, or subtracted, and give a vocabulary clue about each new word.*

Step 3: Generate.

Step 4: Review and reprompt or revise as necessary.

### Prompt Recommendations

- If terms are too complicated, you can reprompt the chatbot to change certain words or clues.

- Tell the bot the types of clues you want (vocabulary, letter changes, word part changes, etc.).

## MAKING CONTENT APPLICABLE

When we give students content that they cannot relate to, we lose them. When an activity is not relatable, student engagement is an uphill battle, even for the most dynamic teachers. For example, fourth-grade teacher Marcus Gray wanted students to practice reading fluency by participating in a Reader's Theatre, performing scripts from grade-level texts. He was excited about the activity and thought it was a perfect way to increase participation in his middle school reading intervention course. Unfortunately, it did not go as planned. When Mr. Gray handed out a Reader's Theatre script created from a well-known fable *The Lion and the Mouse*, his students were anything but excited to join in.

Instead of giving up on the activity altogether, he thought about possible solutions, which included making a relevant script himself or spending time searching for something better. He decided that both options felt time-consuming and unrealistic, so he went to AI for help and entered this prompt:

> *Create a Reader's Theater script for eight participants. Make the setting a middle school in New York. The time of year is winter. Please make it a whole story with a clear problem and solution. Each reader should have at least eight to ten parts in this script.*

Within seconds, he had a script ready to go. Not only was he able to use the script that day, but also after the lesson he was able to ask students what they felt should happen in the next scene, which allowed him to go back to the chatbot to ask it for more scenes to be used in the coming days.

There are plenty of times teachers come across assignments or texts that are simply not applicable or relatable to students. Maybe the assignment was written for learners in a large metropolitan area but your students live in a rural town, or maybe the content feels way too juvenile for readers even when the Lexile level is perfect. Regardless of the reason that the material is not a good fit, AI gives us the ability to make simple adjustments that will make a world of difference when it comes to engaging learners. Rethinking you current teaching techniques with AI in mind might require the willingness to engage in some mental risk-taking, but the suggestions in this playbook can help you get started, and the payoff will be worth it in the end.

## TEACHING ENGAGEMENT

Engagement must be taught, not just expected. Beginning with the youngest students, educators teach students to be active learners by encouraging them to ask questions, respond to peers, advocate when something does not make sense, engage in some form of self-reflection, self-assess their progress, and teach others (e.g., Fisher et al., 2023). Each of these dispositions demonstrates high levels of engagement, but these skills need to be taught.

It is important to note that there are different levels of student engagement. It's not a dichotomy: engaged or disengaged. Berry's Continuum of Engagement (2020) helps analyze the different levels of engagement and offers some simple suggestions for behaviors that educators can teach students to get learners moving from one level to the next (see Figure 9). Specifically, teachers can provide modeling and direct instruction on each level of the engagement continuum and invite students to set their engagement intention and reflect on their actions each day.

**Figure 9** • Continuum of Engagement

| What is my engagement level? | | | | | |
|---|---|---|---|---|---|
| -3 | -2 | -1 | +1 | +2 | +3 |
| Making it hard for others | Off-task | Distracted | Doing my work | Asking questions | Leading others |
| <- | | | | | -> |
| Disrupt | Avoid | Withdraw | Participate | Invest | Drive |
| "Checked-out!" | | | | "Checked-in!" | |

Source: Adapted from Berry (2020) *Disrupting to driving*, Taylor & Francis, and Berry (2022) *Reimagining student engagement*, Corwin.

For example, high school algebra teacher Jessica Goodwin taught students about each level of the continuum and had students ask a bot about behavioral and cognitive behaviors for each level. Each class created posters that summarized their knowledge of each level. Ms. Goodwin starts each class with students setting their engagement intention and checks in with students during the lesson, inviting them to reflect on their level of engagement.

Students refer to this continuum as they are working alongside peers and they use it as a reminder for knowing how to reorient their current level of engagement when it flags. Teachers like Ms. Goodwin can encourage students to use this tool as a reminder to respond to questions, ask questions, or drive their learning by thinking reflectively.

But Ms. Goodwin reported that students don't always know what questions to ask or what comments to share. They want to engage at high levels, but they are not sure what to ask their teacher or peers. Sometimes they are not sure what comments and support they can provide each other. This is another situation where—no surprise—AI can help.

Teaching students how to use AI to prepare for conversations is a great way to support them in using this technology. Before students participate in a group conversation, collaborate on an assignment, or meet in a book club, you can encourage them to visit a chatbot to come up with some questions, prompts, cues, and comments they might want to lean on in the conversation that follows. Ask them to jot down a couple things they could say; whether they use the AI-generated material or not, they will be prepared to participate actively with peers regardless of their comfort level with a topic.

This approach is a great way to encourage students to explore the chatbot tool productively and to model for students that sometimes it takes prompting and patience to get AI to generate something that is most helpful. Engaging in conversation with AI in this way not only gets students ready for discussions and healthy debates with peers but also gets them engaged in thinking about good questions and prompts related to a specific topic up for discussion.

## Classroom Connection

### Get Ready for a Conversation

Step 1: Ask students to visit an assigned chatbot.

Step 2: Have students begin with the request for this AI to help prepare questions, prompts, cues, and comments for an upcoming conversation. For example, they may want to ask for questions to ask about the French Revolution or about the novel they are reading for book club.

Step 3: Ask students to analyze what is generated and revise accordingly with some of the follow-up prompts below:

- Please only give me _____ of each.
- This seems too complicated.
- Can you give me something more specific about _____?
- What is an example answer for these questions?
- This is helpful. Can you give me another example?

Step 4: Remind students that it's appropriate to have several back-and-forth interactions with AI about good questions, prompts, cues, and comments.

Step 5: Engage students in the conversation using the AI-provided supports, and ask them to reflect on the experience.

## Check for Understanding

To check for understanding in this chapter, we have created an assessment using a popular feature of teacher-facing AI sites: the ability to generate true/false statements. Below you will find several true/false statements generated with the help of MagicSchool.ai. Take time to think through each question, applying all you learned about AI and engagement throughout this Educator Function. (See Appendix for answers to all Check for Understanding questions.)

1. True/False: AI tools can help teachers with ideas for building student background knowledge and can be used by students to tap into the background knowledge they already have.

2. True/False: Artificial intelligence can assist educators in making content more relevant and personalized for individual students.

3. True/False: Choice boards are primarily used to give students extra work to complete when they finish another assigned task.

4. True/False: Gaming can be used to make learning enjoyable, memorable, and motivating.

5. True/False: You should avoid having students use AI to plan for conversations with peers because it will take away from their original ideas.

## CONCLUSION

Relevance, motivation, and engagement are important aspects of learning. However, they can be difficult to attain. What works with one class, or one student, may not work with another. As educators, we're on a continual quest to ensure that students engage in meaningful learning. AI can provide resources and ideas that increase the likelihood that students choose to engage. And when students engage, they learn more. And when students engage their teachers' efficacy increases and we feel good about the work we do.

# Educator Function #3

## Meeting Students' Instructional Needs

**EDUCATOR FUNCTION CHALLENGE**

- Customize the learning experiences of students in your class such that they are challenged to do hard things.

Students bring their own interests, talents, background knowledge, and skill set to the classroom each day. Educators not only face the challenge of engaging such a diverse group of students, they also are tasked with the responsibility of teaching every individual, which is no small feat. For the most part, teachers must carefully address the range of student needs day in and day out. This is one of the most challenging parts of the job, and it requires dedicated efforts on the part of the teacher to ensure progress for each learner.

This is not a new challenge in education. In fact, teachers have been required to address the varied needs of their students since there have been schools. The one-room schoolhouse with students across the age span required teachers to meet individual needs and set specific tasks for each learner that would allow them to make progress (Simousek, 2015). And there are laws that protect students with disabilities and ensure that appropriate accommodations and modifications are provided (Jung et al., 2019).

As this challenge continues today, it is likely why books on differentiating instruction are so popular (e.g., Tomlinson & Imbeau, 2023). Educators have learned to differentiate the following:

- Content: The material students need to know and learn

- Process: The activities and experiences students engage in to master content

- Product: The culminating projects, or experiences, where students demonstrate learning

Technologies driven by artificial intelligence hold promise for teachers seeking to differentiate curriculum and instruction in ways that are meaningful, accurate, and consistent with the level of rigor the standards require. However, when misused, without careful review using the teacher's professional judgment, AI can fall far short.

---

### ✎ Stop and Jot

What have been your experiences with managing students' instructional needs?

_____

_____

_____

In what ways have you been able to meet all, or considerably more, of students' varying instructional needs?

_____

_____

_____

Have you worried that expectations for learning outcomes were unintentionally differentiated, resulting in less learning for some students?

_____

_____

_____

---

Knowing ways to adjust the content, process, and product is a starting point, but the real work comes in knowing who your students are, what their strengths are, and where to take them next in their learning journey. While some curriculum resources offer opportunities for customization by including things such as texts at different levels, scaffolds for student access, options for challenging students, and even content in different languages, these resources cannot possibly cover every scenario of need that exists in one classroom.

Often, teachers attempt to meet the needs of individual learners by crafting their own content or materials. This might mean scouring the internet for ideas, spending hours just to make a tool for one group of students, or relying on something a colleague has shared that might be good enough. This conundrum does not arise because teachers don't want to create learning materials that are supportive of students' strengths and needs. Rather, the task itself can be challenging. To do so requires time and thoughtfulness that may not always feel possible with all there is to juggle.

## Ask a Bot

Take time to think about ways AI can be used to customize the learning experiences of students. Using the steps provided, engage in a back-and-forth discussion to consider ways AI can contribute to this important component of learning for teachers and students.

Step 1: Sign in to your favorite chatbot.

Step 2: Ask the chatbot these guiding questions about how it can help with managing students' instructional needs.

- How can AI help teachers manage varying student instructional needs?
- How can AI help customize the learning experiences of _____?
- What are good prompts teachers can use with AI to get differentiated assignments?
- How can AI help teachers to be more efficient when meeting the needs of students?
- What are the risks of relying on AI to help create customized content for differentiation?

Step 3: Engage in a conversation with the chatbot using the *change* or *add on* prompts below.

- *Make that suggestion more concise.*
- *Can you give me an example?*
- *Please explain ...*
- *What would this mean for someone who teaches _____?*
- *What would this mean for a student who is _____?*
- *In my classroom, I need to _____. How could AI help?*

Step 4: Reflect.

- Ahhhhh. I already do this. _____
- AH HA! This is a new idea. _____
- HMMMMM. I'm not so sure about _____.

# ARTIFICIAL INTELLIGENCE AND INSTRUCTIONAL NEEDS

The possibilities AI has shown for automating the process of customizing instruction for all learners has us most excited. It provided the biggest wow factor when we started using AI to meet students' needs, and it tops the celebration when the teachers we work with learn how to use the AI tools in helping with daily teaching functions. In our experience, AI tools respond well to adjusting the custom content a user enters; this process is when the human-like technology shines. Without having to start fresh, AI can alter texts, assignments, directions, and resources with clear and specific prompting.

Additionally, the teacher-facing AI sites have tools designed to help teachers create learning experiences that meet the specific needs of students: tools that provide options for adjusting instructional experiences for students. Figure 10 shows some of the tools available to educators on one teacher-facing site we have mentioned, MagicSchool.ai (www.magicschool.ai).

## Figure 10 • Features on MagicSchool.ai

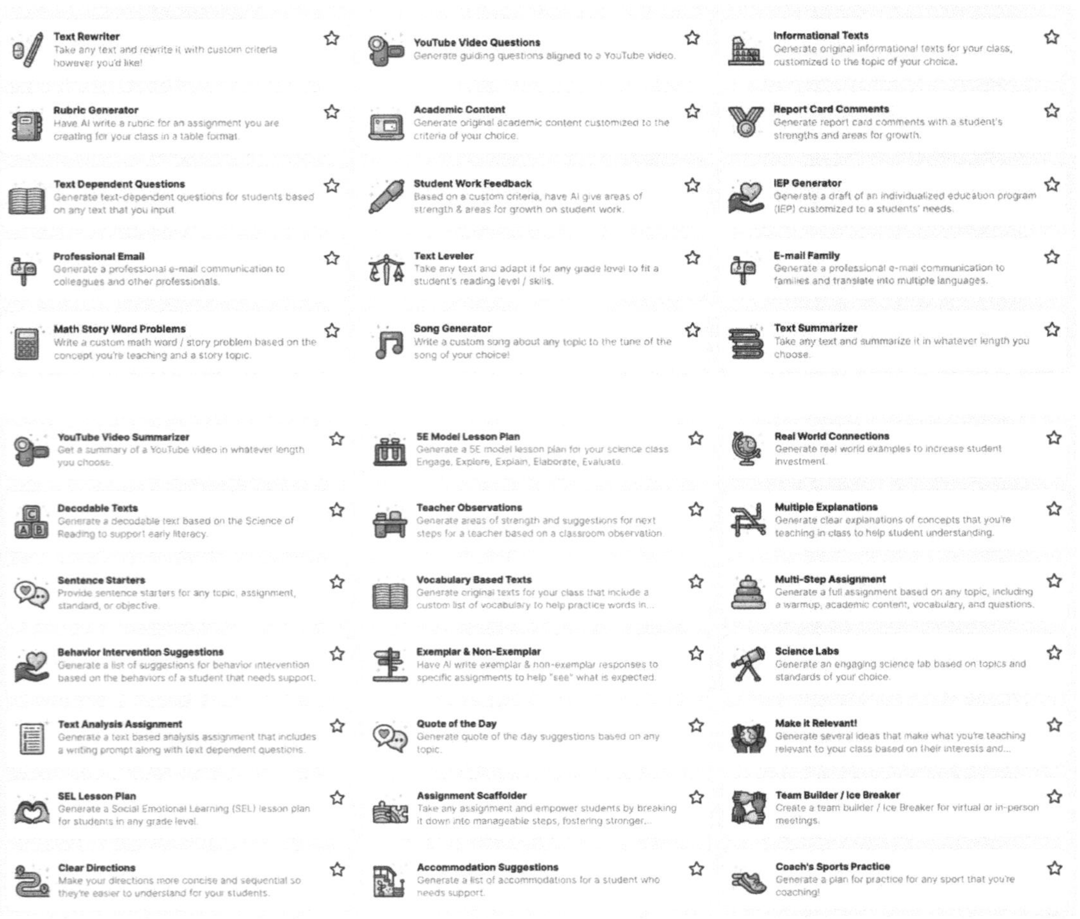

Source: MagicSchool.ai.

## Try It Out!

### Customizing Instruction

. . . . . . . . . . . . . . . . . . . . . . . . . . . . . . . . . . . . . . . . . . . . . . . . . . . . . . . . . . . . . . . . . . . . . . . . . . . . . . .

Look at the features available in Figure 10 and consider ways tools could help you make adjustments in your teaching with specific learners in mind.

- Which of these tools seem most useful for customizing content for your students?

- Which of these tools could take over things you already do to customize content for students?

- Which of these tools would help students access content that might otherwise be too challenging?

- Which of these tools would help you create learning experiences for students who need an extension?

. . . . . . . . . . . . . . . . . . . . . . . . . . . . . . . . . . . . . . . . . . . . . . . . . . . . . . . . . . . . . . . . . . . . . . . . . . . . . . .

There is no doubt you have had to create lessons to meet the needs of individual learners. Maybe you knew adjustments needed to be made to an upcoming lesson. Or maybe you wanted different access points for students you knew might have a hard time understanding the concept you were going to teach. Perhaps you anticipated a possible student struggling with an upcoming assignment and you wanted scaffolds at the ready. The point of creating lessons using the tools explored above is to make content more accessible to a diverse student population.

There is a robust research base on how high-expectations teaching is manifested. This goes beyond statements of belief about children's abilities and potential; high, expectations teaching focuses on the instructional moves of the teacher, which in turn telegraph expectations to students. Expectations are conveyed verbally and nonverbally and impact the socioemotional environment. Importantly, these instructional behaviors are not exclusively aimed at the entire class. In fact, they are often experienced by individual students within the class. In other words, specific students in an otherwise high-expectations classroom may receive a different message of lower expectations. Teacher expectations are conveyed through lesson design, grouping decisions, feedback, questioning, and choice of materials and tasks (Rubie-Davies, 2007). The result of low expectations for an individual student are predictable. Rosenthal and Jacobson (1968) coined the term *The Pygmalion Effect* to describe the impact on achievement when a teacher held either low or high expectations of a child. It comes as no surprise that children experiencing the low expectations of the teacher fail to achieve (Rubie-Davies et al., 2006).

While AI can provide valuable support for differentiating instruction and materials to be used in the classroom, it cannot make up for low-expectations teaching behaviors that are embedded within the teacher's actions. Manifestations of low expectations cool down the learning that might otherwise occur for an individual or group of students (Rubie-Davies, 2007):

- Limit choice and decision making for tasks.

- Repeat directions more frequently than necessary.

- Offer low-level, unsolicited feedback (e.g., reminding a student not to forget a basic cognitive move without evidence that the child would not have done so without the reminder).

- Group lower-achieving students together for long periods of time.

- Infrequently set, discuss, and monitor academic goals.

## Self-Assessment

Use the following self-assessment tool to identify the frequency of the high-expectation practices that you use. Answer each prompt according to the scale 1 = Never, 2 = Rarely, 3 = Sometimes, 4 = Usually, 5 = Always. We invite you to first consider your general teaching style with the entire class. Next, mentally identify a student who is not yet performing at or near grade level. How often do you convey high expectations to this individual?

| How often do you use the following high-expectation practices in your teaching? | | |
|---|---|---|
| | With the Entire Class | With a Student Not Yet Proficient |
| Ask open questions. | | |
| Praise effort rather than correct answers. | | |
| Use regular formative assessment. | | |
| Rephrase questions when answers are incorrect. | | |
| Use mixed-ability groupings. | | |
| Change groupings regularly. | | |
| Encourage students to work with a range of their peers. | | |
| Allow students to choose their own activities from a range of options. | | |
| Make explicit learning intentions and success criteria. | | |
| Allow students to contribute to success criteria. | | |
| Get to know each student personally. | | |
| Incorporate students' interests into activities. | | |
| Regularly review goals with students. | | |
| Minimize differentiation in activities between high and low achievers. | | |

| How often do you use the following high-expectation practices in your teaching? | | |
|---|---|---|
| | **With the Entire Class** | **With a Student Not Yet Proficient** |
| Allow all learners to engage in advanced activities. | | |
| Give specific, instructional feedback about students' achievement in relation to learning goals. | | |
| Manage behavior positively and proactively. | | |
| Work with all students equally. | | |

Source: Adapted from The Education Hub, https://theeducationhub.org.nz/high-expectations-teaching/

A high-expectations teaching orientation paired with responsive curriculum design can result in elevated professional learning community (PLC) team discussions when adjustments are needed. PLCs often focus on studying student data to form a plan for upcoming learning experiences. In our experience, looking to AI for help after studying student data has been a helpful and welcome addition to this common practice.

For example, in preparation for an upcoming unit, a group of sixth-grade teachers brought class sets of student writing to their PLC meeting. The teachers tasked themselves with first sorting the informational writing into three groups: *does not meet standards*, *approaching standards*, and *meeting standards*. Next, they studied each stack, looking to pull out skills they would need to focus on in the unit ahead. They developed three writing skills for each group for use the following week.

| Does Not Meet Standards | Approaching Standards | Meets Standards |
|---|---|---|
| More experience analyzing exemplars and nonexemplars<br><br>Additional instruction about brainstorming and organizing ideas for writing<br><br>More frequent short constructed writing prompts | Sentence starters and transitional phrases to increase academic language<br><br>Additional practice on summarizing and synthesizing content<br><br>Using headings to signal organization | Increased text complexity for writing summaries and precis pieces<br><br>Instruction on analyzing their own work over the semester (Where are you seeing growth? What is still a challenge? What surprised you? How will you meet your goal for next quarter?)<br><br>Teach students about peer response when reading classmate's writing |

At that point, the team turned to AI to get them started. They used AI tools for sentence starters and transitional phrases that could be used with the group of students who were approaching standards. The team had recognized that they could employ students who had meet the standards to provide peer responses to their classmates' writing. They consulted AI to generate best practices for teaching peer response to writing in order to avoid the common trap of students doing low-level mechanics editing on each other's papers. They took advantage of the exemplar and nonexemplar features on a teacher-facing site to create some student tools for the students who did not meet standards.

Next, they turned their attention to developing further accommodations for some of their students with individual education programs (IEP). They loaded the written language accommodations listed on their students' IEPs to create AI prompts to maintain grade level standards rigor with accommodated tasks and texts. (A list of AI supports for students with disabilities appear in Table 3.) At that point, the teachers felt truly inspired about the instruction they would provide for the students in the unit.

**Table 3** • AI Supports for Students With Disabilities

| Tool | Description |
| --- | --- |
| **Tools for Students With Vision-Related Disabilities** | |
| Be My Eyes<br>https://www.bemyeyes.com/ | This AI tool, which is integrated into the Be My Eyes app, offers detailed descriptions of photos to assist blind or visually impaired users. |
| Google AI<br>https://ai.google/ | Google's AI tool describes unlabeled images in multiple languages, aiding those with impaired vision. |
| Image to Text<br>https://www.imagetotext.io/ | This tool provides short, AI-powered descriptions of images. |
| **Tools for Students With Speech- and Hearing-Related Disabilities** | |
| Google's Parrotron | This AI tool, currently in the research stage, helps people with speech-related disabilities convert distorted speech into fluent conversations. |
| Otter.ai<br>https://otter.ai/ | This tool transcribes group conversations. |
| Project Activate<br>https://play.google.com/store/apps/details?id=com.google.android.apps.vision.switches&hl=en_US&gl=US&pli=1 | These communication tools offer supports for nonverbal individuals using facial recognition technology. |
| RogerVoice https://rogervoice.com/en/ | This tool transcribes group conversations. |
| **Tools for Students With Literacy- and Language-Related Disabilities** | |
| Audiopen<br>https://audiopen.ai/ | This tool turns oral input into an organized and well-structured text. |
| MindMeister<br>http://mindmeister.com | This tool helps users visualize and present ideas in an organized fashion. |
| QuillBot<br>https://clickup.com/blog/ai-tools-for-students/ | This AI tool is for notetaking. |
| Speechify Text Reader<br>https://www.orcam.com/en-us/ | This tool converts text into audiobooks, which is beneficial for individuals with dyslexia, ADHD, or sight loss. |

| Tool | Description |
|------|-------------|
| **Tools for Students With Mobility-Related Disabilities** | |
| IFTTT<br>https://ifttt.com/ | This tool automates tasks on apps and devices for those with limited dexterity. |
| Wheelmap<br>https://wheelmap.org | This tool assists mobility-impaired individuals in finding wheelchair-accessible locations. |

Source: Adapted from Disability Horizons Shop (https://shop.disabilityhorizons.com/how-will-ai-help-disabled-people/).

## Task Take-Over

### Supporting Writers

Let's try using one of these tools to convert speech to text and organize the content. Audiopen.ai uses this tagline: "Go from fuzzy thought to clear text. Fast." It is similar to text-to-speech tools you might have used in the past, but it can do so much more. For this take-over, you will step into the shoes of a student who struggles most with writing (specially, a lack of organization when getting ideas on the page).

Step 1: Visit Audiopen.ai and locate the orange microphone button.

Step 2: When you are ready, click the microphone button and give a simple retell of your morning.

Step 3: When you are finished, click the orange square, and let the tool begin generating.

Step 4: After you read the AI-assisted version, you compare it with the original text by clicking the View Original Transcript feature at the bottom of the box.

Source: Audiopen.ai.

*(Continued)*

(Continued)

Now that you have seen this tool in action, consider ways it might support students in your classroom, whether it be those who have language-, literacy-, or processing-related disabilities, or for any student whose writing organization skills are getting in the way of writing. You can teach those students to use this tool as an assistant, and you can help them see how it can help them communicate their original ideas with organization and clarity.

## SUPPORTING LANGUAGE LEARNING

Multilingual learners often spend time in a new school in what is known as the silent period or preproduction phase (e.g., Saville-Troike, 1988). As beginners to a new language, students are taking a lot in, including listening to the pronunciations of the new language, and learning social and cultural norms for the community. But they may not understand much of the content being covered in the class. And they often have a difficult time sharing their thinking with those who do not speak the same languages.

Educators have accepted this silent period as a necessary stage while students develop vocabulary. Often, multilingual learners are paired with others who are more proficient in the language of instruction to provide access to the content as the peer shares what it happening. In other cases, there are paraprofessional staff who speak the languages of students and can provide some access via translation for learners. And, of course, in some schools there are bilingual teachers and biliteracy programs that develop more than one language at the same time.

With that in mind, the silent period does not have to be so silent. There are several AI tools that students can use to provide them with access to the content as their subsequent language skills develop. One such tool that relies on AI is an earbud system that provides bidirectional translation. The Timekettle WT2 Edge language translator, which was the top-rated system at the time of this writing (Best Reviews Guide, 2024), allows users to speak nonstop, and translation will be played in the other person's ear in as little as 0.5 seconds. This is a great AI-driven device to use when a teacher and their multilingual student do not share the same language.

Ximena, a ninth grader who intends to work in the medical field, has strong academic Spanish but is still developing her English proficiency. Her parents relocated to the United States so she could attend a specialty high school that has a health-care pathway. On her first day, the school offered Ximena the translation ear buds, and she was able to access content immediately. As she said, "I thought it would be really hard learning in English, but I understand all of the classes, and I'm working on my English. Also, I am learning new Spanish from the system because we use different words sometimes than the program in my ears uses." Jimena and her teachers don't use it all the time, but instead select it for direct instruction of new content. For her teachers, this device has been transformative. "I'm not always sure if it is language or content knowledge that is interfering. I realized that my experiences with Jimena helped me separate the language demand from the conceptual knowledge," remarked her math teacher.

It's important to note that the language support provided by AI is not only for students at the beginning stage of language development. There are several AI-based translation and image description platforms that provide increased access for learners, such as these:

- Photo Translator: Translates text from images into more than 100 languages

- Pix2Pix: Converts two images to provide comparisons using an AI model for image translation, based on Generative Adversarial Networks (GAN)

- DeepL: Translates documents using a machine translation provider supporting twenty-six languages

- Reverso: Translates vocabulary and dictionary entries for eighteen languages

- Copy.ai: Uses advanced language models for generating copy and translations

- Microsoft Translator: Similar to others listed, this free AI-powered app translates text, speech, and images in over seventy languages

- iTranslate: Supports translation of text, voice, and images in over 100 languages

The other tools we have profiled in this playbook are also useful for multilingual learners. For example, the content-generation tools outlined in Educator Function #3 can be used to customize content for multilingual learners, and the relevance information from Educator Function #4 can be used to ensure that students recognize themselves and their identities in the curriculum.

## Ask a Bot

We've all had the experience of having an idea but not the just-right word to express the concept. A conventional thesaurus gives users lots of synonyms and antonyms for a single word, but it doesn't allow for the use of a phrase or sentence to locate a word. GPTionary.com gives users a word (or more) for what users are thinking. The user provides a descriptive word, phrase, or question, and the tool finds the words that fit the request.

Step 1: Visit gptionary.com.

Step 2: Try this prompt: *Describe a person who is excited for new technology.*

Step 3: Analyze the response. Do you agree with the word choice and options?

Step 4: Try your own word, phrase, or question to generate a word.

Step 5: Introduce this tool to students to help expand their vocabulary.

## ADJUSTING AND CUSTOMIZING TEXTS

Texts can be a major barrier for students at all ages, from those learning to read to those who read well but are challenged with texts that are well above their reading and knowledge levels. When it comes to creating learning experiences that are accessible to all, one of the most important things educators should consider is the complexity of the text they put in front of students. The volume of text, its structural organization, and the vocabulary used significantly influence students' ability to read, engage with, and comprehend the material.

In the past, educators attempted to adjust texts for learners who struggled with the current reading proficiencies by taking these steps:

- Lowering the text complexity levels for some, or all, students

- Having students listen to recorded voices reading the text to them

- Selecting excerpts that allowed students a sample of text but not the entirety of it

Interestingly, as a text- and language-based system, most AI tools require input (written or spoken) to produce new written output. This, in turn, can actually increase the reading demand. Of course, the generated text can be read aloud or paired down, but the receiver still must understand it and be able to process the information. And AI can produce much more condensed versions, which is both positive and negative. It's positive when students have access to the ideas and information, but it's negative if their overall reading volume declines, because reading volume is strongly correlated with overall achievement (Fisher & Frey, 2018).

Think about directions you have included on a recent assignment, the explanations you have shared at the start of a math lesson, or even criteria you have included in a rubric. These are all types of text educators present to students, which they are expected to read, understand, and take action. In these situations, AI tools can help. With the correct prompting, they have the ability to change and adapt texts based on what teachers are looking for and what students need.
Table 4 highlights some of the potential adjustments in text demands that can be accomplished with AI.

## Table 4 • Adjustments in Text Demands

| Adjustment | Suggested Prompt |
| --- | --- |
| Volume | • Consolidate this text to make it _____ paragraphs.<br>• Summarize this passage.<br>• Make a shorter version of the text below.<br>• Highlight the main ideas in the passage. |
| Organization | • Rewrite _____ in steps.<br>• Break the text into _____ parts.<br>• Highlight _____ to make it easier to understand. |
| Vocabulary | • Change the following words: _____, _____, _____.<br>• Simplify the vocabulary.<br>• Create a mini-glossary for the text.<br>• Provide definitions for the following terms: _____, _____, _____. |

In addition to using these prompts in general AI sites, educators can use the text-leveling tools included in many teacher-facing AI sites to adjust text complexity with very little input. With that in mind, it's important to note that we have found that these tools can accurately make texts easier *and* more challenging. What can be sacrificed is what is referred to as text cohesion, which is the extent to which the ideas within and across sentences hang together. Text engineered for school-age readers typically rely on lots of transitional phrases and context clues, such as providing an embedded definition of word or using a familiar synonym or example to further explain an idea. A text that has been shortened to improve readability might delete some of these features, thus making the text less comprehensible to your students. When converting text, always make sure to read it closely yourself to see if the text remains cohesive. There is no substitute for the human in the loop when it comes to carefully screening text.

Clearly, there is still room for improvement in terms of AI's current ability to precisely align the text it generates with a particular grade level. And again, we caution teachers that simply making the texts easier is not the answer. It's the instruction—including the questions, prompts, and cues that we provide—that can support students in reading increasingly complex texts. Fortunately, AI can help us generate those questions, prompts, and cues so that our students are engaged in meaningful learning.

## Try It Out!

### Adjusting Texts

Step 1: Find an example of text you want to adjust.

Step 2: Visit the teacher-facing site www.magicschool.ai.

Step 3: Select the Magic School Text-Leveler Tool.

Step 4: Fill in required fields: grade level and text.

Step 5: Generate.

Step 6: Review text for content, clarity, and voice.

Step 7: Make revisions and adjustments as needed.

## CUSTOMIZING SCAFFOLDS AND SUPPORTS

Scaffolding is any temporary instructional practice a teacher uses to improve a student's access to concepts, skills, and texts. Common material scaffolds include providing language frames, graphic organizers, or parallel math problems. Other scaffolds are teacher driven, such as modeling and thinking aloud, and furnishing prompts and cues when a student is stuck. Scaffolds can be considered before a lesson occurs, during the lesson, or after the lesson (Frey et al., 2023).

There are benefits and risks in placing scaffolds in any of these positions. For example, front-end scaffolds, also known as just-in-case, run the risk of reducing rigor for students. Supplying a list of new vocabulary words and definitions in advance of a reading is an example of a front-end scaffold. But without them, some students will experience failure. Distributed scaffolds (during the lesson) are also known as just-in-time scaffolds, and they can be useful in maintaining rigor but may also require that students experience repeated failures before receiving support. Teacher prompting a cueing is an example of a distributed scaffold, as it occurs in response to an interaction with the student. Back-end scaffolds come after the learning experience, such as asking students to develop a graphic organizer to summarize the concepts in the lesson. There is no perfect scaffold—or time to scaffold—that will ensure that all students learn.

As with other demands on teachers, scaffolding remains a challenge for addressing the individual needs of learners in their class. That may mean that all students receive the same scaffolds, regardless of whether or not they need them or can use them. Here, too, the situation is sometimes limited by the reality of time and planning. As educators, we tend to select the most useful scaffolds to ensure that most students are learning.

There are several ways AI can help with scaffolding. For instance, it can create guiding questions for a lengthy text so students can check for understanding along the way. Not only does this additional support save teachers time, but also they can allocate that time to responding to students who are confused by the questions. Here are some of the creative ways in which teachers have used AI to develop scaffolds.

- Outlining a longer text to help students with note-taking

- Providing lists of sentence starters to support a collaborative discussion among students

- Giving ideas for graphic organizers that match the assignment

- Producing a template students can follow for a written response

- Creating a list of vocabulary terms and accompanying definitions for a text

## CUSTOMIZING INTERVENTIONS

Regardless of the grade level or subject area—and irrespective of district policy, requirements, and norms for student-progress monitoring—the implementation of classroom interventions is a crucial aspect of effective teaching. While formal intervention processes may vary depending on the situation, all educators face this question: "What can I do to help this learner who has shown the need for extra support?"

As we have already addressed, each learner presents a unique challenge, and the more customized the intervention, the more likely it is to succeed. Interventions work best when they are thoughtfully designed with a particular learner or group of learners in mind. To identify ways to provide extra support, teachers might consider using a tool or technique that has worked in the past, asking colleagues for suggestions, or turning to AI, which can eliminate the delays that typically occur when teachers must wait for a colleague or coach to be available.

In our experience, AI tools can serve as an effective thought partner in generating ideas about possible interventions. Teachers can input specific data, student needs, interventions that have not worked, and the standard being addressed, and AI has the ability to produce a list of research-based options to choose from. Although this process can be done using general AI sites like ChatGPT, Bard, or Claude, we have found that in this instance, using teacher-facing sites Eduaide.ai or Curipod.ai, which are better equipped with knowledge of standards and teaching practices, is more effective.

For example, one of the Teaching Assistant tools on Eduaide.ai is designed to generate lists of targeted, evidence-based interventions to address specific student needs. The tool, Evidence-Based Interventions, prompts teachers to enter grade level, standards, and any additional specific details they want the technology to keep in mind. Within seconds it offers a list of intervention ideas and includes references to the research base for the suggestion. We tried it out to generate ideas we could use to help a middle school student who needs support with reading comprehension on any task that requires them to read a passage independently. The figure below shows generated results, which focuses on a sample study or resource and the topic, such as repeated reading or comprehension instruction. These ideas would have to be further investigated and explored by educators. We expect that the resources on interventions will expand as more educators ask for them.

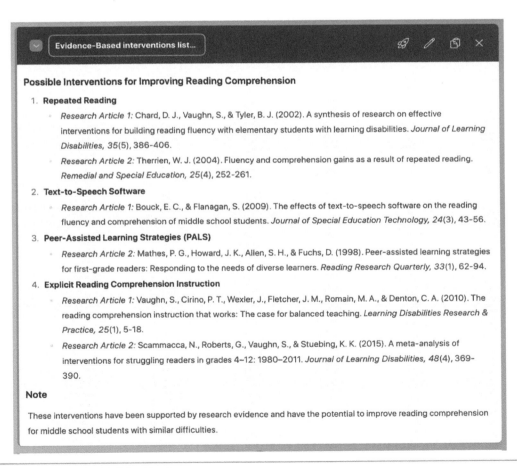

Source: Generated with Eduaide.ai.

As with everything we have addressed thus far, users have the responsibility to look carefully at the output and should consider the credibility of sources provided. Even though there are suggestions that might be less effective than others, this is a starting point and a chance for users to build knowledge of research-based strategies to implement as interventions in the classroom.

## Check for Understanding

With the content of this Educator Function in mind, take some time to check for understanding using the multiple-choice questions below, using an AI tool to develop them. (See Appendix for answers to all Check for Understanding questions.)

Question 1: What are the three areas in which educators should consider customizing learning experiences for students?

   a) Content, process, and product

   b) Reading, writing, and arithmetic

   c) Assessment, lesson planning, and feedback

   d) Classroom management, technology integration, and communication

Question 2: What is one way in which AI can support students with literacy-related disabilities?

   a) Providing access to translated texts

   b) Generating vocabulary quizzes

   c) Creating recordings of themselves reading

   d) Offering grammar correction exercises

Question 3: What is the purpose of the "Magic School Text-Leveler Tool" mentioned in the Educator Function?

   a) To auto-generate lesson plans

   b) To adjust the complexity of texts

   c) To create digital flashcards

   d) To facilitate peer editing

Question 4: How can AI help teachers create scaffolds for students?

   a) By providing lists of sentence starters

   b) By grading student assignments

   c) By conducting parent-teacher conferences

   d) By organizing field trips

Question 5: What is a key consideration when implementing classroom interventions, as mentioned in the Educator Function?

a) Implementing interventions without teacher input

b) Using the same intervention for all students

c) Thoughtfully designing interventions with a particular learner or group of learners in mind

d) Implementing interventions based on district policy only

## CONCLUSION

In Educator Function #3, we focused on the ways in which content can be customized. But teaching our students involves much more than sharing the content; great teachers make the content come alive. With that in mind, teachers are frequently challenged by the range of needs, interests, and skills of the students in their classrooms. We run the risk of running out of time while trying to meet every need and ensure that every student is challenged by the lessons we design. We selected the AI tools highlighted in this chapter to help you address that reality and provide you with access to resources you may have not had before. We hope you will continue to turn to AI for additional assistance as you customize the learning experiences of the unique students in your classes.

# Educator Function #4

## Assessing Student Learning

Assessment, which is another essential function of teachers, serves as an important factor in connecting teaching and learning. There are hundreds of books and articles that provide perspectives on what types of assessments should be used and when. Most instructional materials and curriculum resources include assessment. In fact, each reader of this playbook comes with their own understanding of what assessment is and what assessment looks like in their classroom, school, or district. As a reminder, the word *assessment* comes from the Latin *assidere*, which means "to sit beside," which suggests that we use assessment tools to guide teaching as well as evaluate learning.

Assessment development is time consuming, yet we need good information and evidence from students to make instructional decisions and report student progress to students and their families or caregivers. AI can help in the development of assessment tools. As we have noted many times in this playbook, AI generates a draft or some ideas that educators need to review and revise. Again, the 80/20 rule comes to mind. Make sure that the assessments that are AI generated meet your needs and adequately assess the concepts you find most valuable.

But AI is not limited to assessment development. There are a number of tools that you can use to interpret the evidence that is collected. AI can create visualizations of the data that are helpful in making decisions about where to go next with students by providing feedback comments on student work, using criteria that are established in advance. Again, you will need to consider the feedback offered by AI and customize that for your students.

---

### ✎ Stop and Jot

What are some examples of assessments you have created, administered, and evaluated?

_____

_____

Which example was the most time-consuming for you to create, administer, or implement?

_____

_____

What assessments gave you the best information?

_____

_____

What would you like to do differently with any of these assessments moving forward?

_____

_____

---

We recognize that assessments come in different shapes and sizes; we also realize that it is best to look beyond a perfect definition of *assessment* to examine closely instead what benefits assessments can provide to students and teachers. Whatever the type, however it is defined, an assessment is essentially a tool for measuring and evaluating student learning in a way that captures information about the skills students have or have yet to master. Ultimately assessment is the function of teaching where educators gather information, report progress, and make decisions about future teaching.

---

### Ask a Bot

Take time to think about ways AI can be used to support assessment in the classroom. Using the steps provided, engage in a back-and-forth around ways AI can support classroom assessment practices and consider ways the technology can help us reimagine this necessary educator function.

---

Step 1: Sign in to your favorite chatbot.

Step 2: Ask the chatbot these guiding questions about how it can help with assessment:

- *In what ways can AI assist with classroom assessments?*

- *How will AI be able to help educators create assessments?*

- *What should teachers keep in mind when using AI to create assessments?*

- *How will AI help educators reimagine assessment in the classroom?*

- *What AI tools and features will help most with classroom assessment?*

Step 3: Engage in a conversation with the chatbot using the change or add on prompts below.

- *Make that suggestion more concise.*

- *Consolidate the response to one big idea.*

- *Can you give me an example?*

- *Please explain ...*

- *What would this mean for someone who teaches _____?*

- *I have a student who _____. What would this mean for them?*

Step 4: Reflect.

- Ahhhhh. I already do this. _____

- AH HA! This is a new idea. _____

- HMMMMM. I'm not so sure about _____.

The challenges that educators have with assessment include the time it takes teachers to create, administer, and evaluate them, coupled with the task of then planning instruction based on the interpretation of the assessment's data. When done well, assessments provide teachers with specific information about the students in front of them. However, from year to year, the information a teacher seeks could change depending on data, student groupings, school or district goals, or even the timing of a unit. This can be a significant undertaking, potentially limiting the way assessments might inform teaching due to the complexities involved. In this Educator Function, we focus on the ways in which AI can help with the development of assessments and the evaluation of the data obtained from these assessments.

## Self-Assessment

*Consider the following aspects of assessment and rate yourself. What areas do you want to strengthen? How might AI help?*

| Aspects of Relevance (adapted from Fisher et al., 2023) | |
| --- | --- |
| I have sufficient time to create assessment tools. | |
| I have sufficient expertise to create assessment tools. | |
| I have sufficient time to administer assessments. | |
| I have sufficient time to evaluate and interpret assessments. | |
| I have sufficient expertise to evaluate and interpret assessments. | |
| I have sufficient time to plan instruction based on the information gained from the assessments. | |
| I have sufficient expertise to plan instruction based on the information gained from the assessments. | |

## DEVELOPING ASSESSMENT TASKS

Phil Petersen, a sixth-grade math teacher in Connecticut, wanted to see what his students had mastered toward the end of the unit on the order of operations. This was his fifteenth year teaching sixth grade and his fifteenth time teaching order of operations at this level. The assessment he was planning to use was the same one he had used for years, and it was one that he found usually gave a decent amount of information about student learning.

However, when Phil reviewed the assessment again, he realized that the first page of the assessment was mostly about what order of operations was, something he already knew his students had mastered. Phil decided to use ChatGPT to assist in revising the assessment to focus on the information he most wanted to know about his students. He quickly quick copied and pasted the assessment into the AI tool and then used this prompt: *Please adjust this assessment so that it primarily focuses on students' application of parentheses and exponents.* Seconds later, he had an assessment that was specific to the needs of the group.

In the earlier chapters and Educator Functions, we have explored ways AI can generate content that can be assessed. In fact, at the end of each chapter, you have experienced examples of ways AI can create simple "Check for Understanding" assessments, including multiple-choice, fill-in-the-blank, and true/false questions, along with more open-ended options like discussion questions and scenarios for application. Both the general AI tools and the teacher-facing tools support creating new or modifying existing assessments.

When you are creating and modifying assessments, you have an opportunity to think carefully about the content being assessed, the type of assessment used, and the format of the assignment itself. Each of these elements impacts the evidence generated by the assessment. With these possibilities in mind, take some time to consider ways AI can help you with existing assessment practices. Some common assessment types are listed in Table 5. Rethinking your current assessment techniques with AI in mind might require some thinking outside the box and mental risk-taking, but it will be well worth it to ensure that the evidence collected from students about their learning is useful.

**Table 5** • Common Assessment Types

| Assessment Type | How It Works | Effective Uses |
|---|---|---|
| Unit Assessment | A task or set of questions are designed around all skills addressed during a particular unit of study. | Measuring mastery and understanding at the culmination of time dedicated to a particular topic |
| Universal Response | All students respond to a question or prompt simultaneously, using gestures or tools such as a whiteboard or online response platform. | Efficiently assessing understanding and engaging all students in thinking and responding |
| Exit Tickets | Students are given a short assignment—usually in the form of a question or quick check-in—and respond accordingly. | Assessing the understanding of or progress toward a particular learning objective or success criteria |
| Teach-Back | Students engage in teaching someone else (e.g., a partner, table group, or class) what they know or what they learned. | Giving students the chance to articulate and synthesize prior knowledge or learning while giving the teacher insight into understanding |
| Quantitative Check-In | A reflection question is presented (e.g., *How sure are you of this answer?* or *How deep was your understanding?*), and students quantify their reflection on a 1–10 scale. | Quantifying student reflections in a way that provides specific data on students who might need support or clarification |
| Oral Response | Students engage in a discussion around a particular topic, question, or scenario, and the conversation is recorded and analyzed. | Making an assessment accessible to learners who might struggle with written work and providing data not just on the topic being discussed but also on speaking and listening skills used |
| Rubrics and Checklists | Teachers, often in collaboration with students, identify indicators that need to be addressed and then create a proficiency scale that articulates levels of success. | Identifying areas that need additional instructional attention and using these tools for students to self-assess or provide peer feedback |

The various types of assessments listed each have their pros and cons. There is no perfect assessment tool, and the format we choose will inherently have its own limitations. You may have noticed that conundrum in the checks for understanding portion of the Educator Functions in this playbook. We left them just as AI generated them so that you could see these authentic examples. Of course, when we use assessments with students, we revise them to ensure that they are the best possible tools for collecting evidence from students. Table 6 contains some example assessment formats and the pros and cons for each.

**Table 6** • Pros and Cons of Assessment Formats

| Assessment Format | Pros | Cons |
|---|---|---|
| Multiple Choice | • Efficient administration<br>• Objective scoring<br>• Broad content coverage | • Potential guessing<br>• Lack of critical thinking<br>• Feedback to students limited |
| True/False | • Straightforward<br>• Quick fact recall<br>• Accessible | • Potential guessing<br>• Lack of critical thinking<br>• Oversimplification |
| Fill-in-the-Blank | • Assesses associations<br>• Supports vocabulary skills<br>• Serves as content review | • Limited context<br>• Suggests one answer<br>• Puts multi-language learning (MLL) students at disadvantage |
| Short Response Questions | • Assesses understanding of skill<br>• Provides insight into student thinking<br>• Requires evidence and explanation<br>• Assesses structure of written response | • Dependent on understanding of one question<br>• Subjective scoring<br>• Time-consuming for students and teachers |
| Project Based | • Opportunity for real-world application<br>• Provides insight into student thinking<br>• Encourages creativity<br>• Individualized | • Potential to focus on format or design over content<br>• Subjective scoring<br>• Time-consuming for students and teachers |

## Task Takeover

### Developing Assessment Tools

Take some time to reflect on the techniques you use to assess students in your classroom. These can be examples specific to one lesson or unit or things that are a regular part of your daily practice.

Examples of your assessment techniques:

1. _____

2. _____

3. _____

4. _____

5. _____

6. _____

Looking critically at that list, use the chart that follows to think about how AI might help.

| Examples of Assessments | Ways AI Can Support Them |
|---|---|
| Our Example: Comprehension question about character development based on a read aloud.<br><br>The teacher is reading aloud *Shiloh* (Naylor, 1991) and wants students to track the way Marty changes based on the experiences he has. | AI can create standards-aligned questions that can give teachers the data they want by entering a specific standard and the text into AI and asking it to generate a few question options accordingly.<br><br>• Are there any supporting characters in the novel who have an influence on the main character's development?<br><br>• Are there any moments in the story where the main character shows courage or kindness?<br><br>• How would you describe the main character's personality at the beginning of the story? How has it changed at this point? |
| Our Example: Students are learning about stoichiometry and the teacher wants to assess the ability to balance chemical reactions. | AI can create a set of problems such as the following:<br><br>1. Given the unbalanced equation, $C_4H_{10} + O_2 \rightarrow CO_2 + H_2O$, balance it, and then calculate how many moles of oxygen ($O_2$) are needed to completely react with 2 moles of propane ($C_4H_{10}$).<br><br>2. Balance the equation for the reaction between potassium chlorate ($KClO_3$) and hydrogen peroxide ($H_2O_2$) to form potassium chloride ($KCl$) and oxygen ($O_2$). |
| Your Example: | |

# AI-RESISTANT ASSESSMENTS

When educators first learn about AI and consider the impact it will have on education, a frequent concern they share with us involves students using the technology to effortlessly—and inauthentically—answer questions and complete assignments. There is valid apprehension about the use of AI to game the system or "cheat" on assignments and assessments, given the ease with which students can answer and complete some tasks using technology. This realization should encourage a reevaluation of the nature of the tasks, assignments, and assessments themselves. Rather than focusing on the potential misuse of AI, we encourage you to see this as an invitation to reflect on the types of assessments we currently use, and the depth of learning and understanding they have the potential to show.

Adeel Khan, founder of MagicSchool.ai, spoke about AI-resistant assessments in a webinar hosted by AI for Education. He talked about the ways in which educators can rethink assessments and create tasks, assignments, and measures of learning that not only alleviate the temptation for students to cut corners but ultimately generate the type of data and information teachers need to analyze student proficiency. Khan went on to discuss the current technological revolution as an opportunity to think about what we are currently doing and how it might change for the better.

Based on the concept of AI-resistant assessments, we have spent time considering the types of tools we use in classrooms. Table 7 contains examples of assessments that are considered AI-Resistant and others that are not. As you look at the list, note that there are types of assessments that are harder to answer with AI. These are not new assessment formats, but rather applications of ideas that require students to generate their own responses. Note that we use the term AI-resistant, not AI-proof. It is possible for AI to assist with some of these assessment tools, but they do require more complexity of thinking on the part of learners. Interestingly, AI can help with AI-Resistant Assessments. For example, it's easy for AI to generate a list of authentic, real-world applications.

**Table 7 •** AI-Resistant and Non-Resistant Assessment Formats

| AI-Resistant Assessments | Non–AI-Resistant Assessments |
| --- | --- |
| Open-ended questions | Multiple-choice questions |
| Application of different perspectives | True/False statements |
| Problem-solving tasks | Fill-in-the-blank tasks |
| Critical-thinking exercises | Basic vocabulary assessments |
| Authentic, real-world applications | Simple recall tasks |
| Debate or oral assessments | Formulaic tasks |

## Try It Out!

### Addressing Assessment Resistance

Using the chart that follows, reflect on a few of the assessments you currently use in your teaching. Consider how AI-resistant your current assessments are, and take some time to identify changes you might make in the future to get a more in-depth view of student knowledge and application.

| Assessment Tool | Level of AI-Resistance (1–5) | Possible Changes |
|---|---|---|
| | 1 = Students could easily use AI tools to complete the task.<br><br>5 = AI tools would not assist students in completion of the task. | |
| Our Example: Multiple-choice assessment from Educator Function #1 | 1 | • Add a requirement that students support their answer with a narrative response.<br>• Ask students to explain why the distractors are incorrect.<br>• Have students generate additional distractors based on the information they know.<br>• Provide the answers and have students justify why they are correct. |
| | | |
| | | |

Of course, there is a time and place for the assessments that fall under the Non-AI Resistant category. We have used a range of AI-resistant and less resistant tools in the checks for understanding for each Educator Function. When you want to rapidly check for understanding, especially in-person, the non-resistant tools can provide evidence. Don't let the principle of AI-Resistant assessment discourage you from considering the circumstances in which you can collect student data. However, use these ideas to rethink current practices and ways this technology can propel you toward new—or strengthened—assessments that require students to showcase different aspects of learning.

## ASSESSMENTS OF TRANSFER

Students' ability to carry learning with them from one context to another is the best way to see their mastery of a skill, and this capability should be the end goal of all learning. Wiggins (2013) describes it this way: "Transfer means that a learner can draw upon and apply from all of what was learned, as the situation warrants." After all, the point of learning is for students to acquire skills and knowledge that they can use in situations where the teacher is no longer present.

Assessing our students' ability to transfer skills and knowledge is an effective way we can evaluate their overall understanding of a concept and their ability to apply skills and knowledge independently. Notably, transfer tasks even highlight misconceptions and misunderstandings that can be retaught. Fisher, Frey, and Hattie (2016) noted that learning should progress from surface, to deep, to transfer (see Figure 11). But that only happens when tasks and learning strategies align with those phases of learning.

**Figure 11** • Phases of Learning

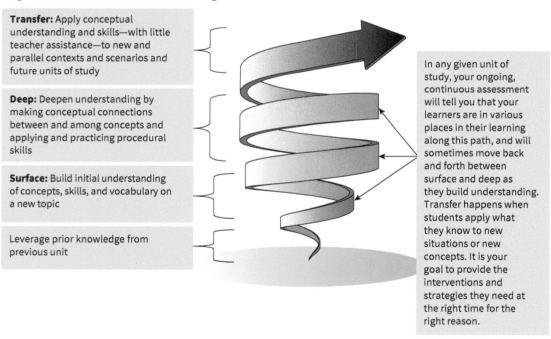

**Transfer:** Apply conceptual understanding and skills—with little teacher assistance—to new and parallel contexts and scenarios and future units of study

**Deep:** Deepen understanding by making conceptual connections between and among concepts and applying and practicing procedural skills

**Surface:** Build initial understanding of concepts, skills, and vocabulary on a new topic

Leverage prior knowledge from previous unit

In any given unit of study, your ongoing, continuous assessment will tell you that your learners are in various places in their learning along this path, and will sometimes move back and forth between surface and deep as they build understanding. Transfer happens when students apply what they know to new situations or new concepts. It is your goal to provide the interventions and strategies they need at the right time for the right reason.

Source: Hattie et al., 2016.

Many assessments provide information about skill acquisition at the early phases of learning. For example, a multiple-choice set of questions might show students' understanding of concepts. Open-ended questions can be designed as opportunities for students to show deeper understanding and apply skills. An end-of-unit test or on-demand writing task can demonstrate transfer. That said, the idea of transfer is not just about applying skills a few weeks later. Rather, transfer requires that students can apply skills and knowledge in new contexts and during different experiences.

Assessments that truly measure transfer, which is the final phase of learning, are harder to come by. AI can assist in generating learning experiences and assessment tasks that require transfer as a way for teachers to measure this level of understanding. Here are some of the tasks we have found best measure transfer:

- *Authentic Scenarios*: These are assignments that present real-world scenarios, requiring students to apply learned skills in practical contexts. For instance, imagine that students have just finished a math unit on finding area. The teacher gives them a scenario about a group of students who want to make a garden for the school, and the learners have to apply the knowledge they've learned about area to complete the assigned task.

- *Application to Content Area*: These are opportunities for students to take a skill they have learned in one subject area and apply it in another. For instance, imagine that in reading, students have been learning to find the main idea and supporting details of expository nonfiction texts, and in science they have been learning about weather. While the class is reading about the causes of severe weather in science, the teacher asks students to find the main idea and supporting details of one of the passages shared.

- *Performance Tasks*: These are assignments that are used to assess students' knowledge, understanding, and proficiency. Performance tasks result in product or performance that serve as evidence of learning. For example, students may be asked to present on a topic, engage in a debate, or produce a product.

- *Simulations*: These are interactive assignments that require students to apply multiple skills they have learned to complete a task. Imagine that students have finished a lesson from the school's SEL curriculum on trust. The teacher pairs them with a partner, and while one partner is blindfolded, the other partner has to take them on a walk around the school. The partner must give full trust that their classmate will lead them safely.

- *Revision of Previous Work*: This task involves revisiting a past assignment or past work with new learning in mind. Imagine that students have just learned about word endings. The teacher assigns them to go back to a letter they wrote to the teacher in the first days of school and edit it for word endings. In a different color, the students rewrite words that end in *-ing*, *-ed*, or *-ies*, using the new learning.

We have found that prompting general AI sites to help create some of the transferable assessment experiences suggested above has given teachers ideas to incorporate in lessons and units. When you ask AI to assist with these ideas, be sure to include the time you have available to administer the assessment so the generated result is a good match for what you need. As an example, when Jane Donovan, a second-grade teacher on Long Island, first asked ChatGPT to create a simulation for students to practice what they had learned about forces and motion, it gave an applicable idea but one that would take weeks to complete. Jane quickly adjusted the prompt to include *Suggest a thirty-minute simulation*, and within seconds she received an idea that felt useful.

# INTERPRETING DATA

In Educator Function #5, we talked about the importance of looking closely at data to make plans for future instruction, and we suggested that AI can assist in the thoughtful development of these plans. In that Educator Function, we included a passage about a group of sixth-grade teachers who were looking at a stack of student work and sorting it while thinking about instructional needs in the unit ahead. The practice of looking closely at student work is an important one, and it is not something we suggest completely handing over to AI. However, in Educator Function #5 we also shared ways that AI tools can help interpret and analyze data. In fact, it can even provide another perspective or additional insight on the evidence. Also, AI can help teachers automate the process of organizing data in a way that makes the study of the data more efficient.

Let's consider another example of AI assisting in the analysis of student assessment data. Kindergarten teachers are tasked with teaching letters and sounds: letter identification, letter formation (upper and lower), letter names, and letter sounds. With an average of twenty-two students in a classroom, twenty-six letters, and all these categories, it is an incredible amount of information to track. Yet for these educators, it is essential not only to keep track of what students have mastered but also to be referencing this data on a daily basis in order to be sure each student is practicing the specific skill they are approximating.

A group of kindergarten teachers in Saint Louis recently used AI to create a form they can update weekly and keep with them during a literacy block to coach students accordingly. Previously, the teachers did this by hand, going through each spreadsheet and adding what each student needed to work on next to their name. With AI, they are now able to input the tables they use and keep track of all categories of letter and sound knowledge. They have also developed prompts that allow AI to create a table with each student's name and what the student needs to work on. Clearly, the ability of these tools to automate a task that is essential to this grade level and area of study is a huge win, and it gives teachers back the hours they were having to spend to manually interpret this data on their own.

## Classroom Connection

### Goal Setting

Step 1: Ask students to visit an assigned chatbot.

Step 2: Assign students to focus on a particular piece of work that you know will be helpful for goal setting (e.g., a written response to a comprehension question, a portion of an essay, a math explanation, or steps taken to complete an assignment).

Step 3: Ask students to enter the work and prompt the bot with the following questions:

- *What am I doing well?*
- *What should I do next?*
- *What is working?*
- *What is not working?*

Step 4: Ask students to read and analyze the output. Then task them with drafting three possible goals.

Step 5: Ask students to draft goals into the bot and ask it for feedback with these questions:

- *What do you think about these goals?*
- *Based on the answers you gave above, which of these goals should I focus on first?*

Step 6: Have students engage in one more round of questioning with the bot, asking it for assistance in making a three-step plan for how to work toward the main goal.

Step 7: Have students talk about the responses they are getting from the bot by analyzing the advice it is giving, talking about accuracy, or even comparing and contrasting output with peers.

## Check for Understanding

To check for understanding in this Educator Function, answer the following fill-in-the-blank questions, which were created with the assistance of AI. These questions are intended to help you think through the ways AI can support teachers in classroom assessment. (See Appendix for answers to all Check for Understanding questions.)

1) Assessment is an essential function of teachers and serves as an important factor in connecting _____ and _____.

2) Universal Response assessments are useful for assessing _____ and engaging all students in thinking and _____.

3) AI-resistant assessments encourage educators to rethink the nature of tasks and focus on obtaining data points that show the _____ of student understanding, knowledge, and application.

4) Assessments of Transfer focus on students' ability to carry learning from one context to another, which is considered the best way to demonstrate _____ of a skill.

5) The ability of AI tools to automate essential tasks, such as data interpretation, is described as a significant win for teachers, giving them back _____.

## CONCLUSION

Assessment of student learning, which can be used for reporting information and for making instructional decisions, is a critical task that educators must complete on a regular basis. Generating assessment ideas takes time, but AI can help. In addition, AI can assist teachers with the analysis of the data, even organizing the data or creating visual data displays. By using AI, teachers can adapt and adopt assessments more quickly and get to the business of providing high-quality instruction based on the evidence collected.

# Educator Function #5

## Providing Effective Feedback

Feedback, which plays a crucial role in the process of learning and academic achievement, can provide learners with direction, and help them navigate a path forward. For educators, the significance of providing feedback is not a new concept; it is an essential part of the job. Few would dispute how important feedback is and why it is frequently covered in academic publications, curriculum resources, and professional development sessions. However, while its importance is known, it can also be one of the most challenging aspects of the job.

The type of feedback and the way the feedback is given can make a profound difference on its impact. According to Wiśniewski et al. (2020), feedback has the potential to have a powerful effect on student learning, but its overall effectiveness is influenced by a handful of variables:

*Timeliness.* For feedback to be useful, educators are urged to deliver it promptly—before it becomes stale and while it is still applicable to student learning.

*The type of feedback provided.* When feedback is specific and actionable, students are most likely to make it a part of their learning process.

*The specificity of information given.* General comments or suggestions are less useful as students are often unsure what to do next. Too specific information removes the responsibility from students, and they simply comply and do what the teacher tells them, not learning in the process.

It can be challenging for teachers to balance these factors and to navigate the reality of just how much feedback is required. Throughout this Educator Function, we will explore how AI can help.

---

### ✎ Stop and Jot

What type of feedback do you currently provide to students?

1. _____
2. _____
3. _____
4. _____
5. _____

Which of these are the most useful?

_____

_____

_____

If you had more time, what would you add to your feedback repertoires?

_____

_____

_____

---

## ARTIFICIAL INTELLIGENCE FOR FEEDBACK

Using artificial intelligence for feedback is not a new concept. Adaptive technology and automated systems have played a role in grading and assessment for many years. There are plenty of adaptive benchmark assessments that provide teachers and students with real-time feedback in the form of scores or learning pathways specific to individual needs. These automated assessments can be effective in identifying needs and reducing the amount of time spent on assessments. But AI can do more. In this Educator Function, we focus on the ways in which AI can help educators with the content of their feedback.

Although AI tools do not replace the need for teacher–student interactions or the important role that live, in-the-moment feedback plays, they can play a helpful role as a type of assistant coach. These tools lack the depth of knowledge a teacher has about students and the content being taught, but they can still provide a starting point and help improve the overall efficiency of the feedback process.

## Ask a Bot

Take time to think about ways AI can be used for feedback in education. Using the steps provided, engage in back-and-forth to consider ways AI can contribute to this important component of learning for teachers and students.

Step 1: Sign into your favorite chatbot.

Step 2: Ask the chatbot guiding questions about how it can help with feedback.

- *How can AI help teachers with feedback?*

- *What are effective ways to use AI when giving feedback?*

- *What are important things to consider when using AI to help with teacher feedback?*

- *Can AI be helpful in giving students feedback?*

Step 3: Engage in a conversation with the chatbot using these *change* or *add-on* prompts.

- *Make that suggestion more concise.*

- *Consolidate the response to one big idea.*

- *Can you give me an example?*

- *Please explain _____.*

- *What would this mean for someone who teaches _____?*

- *What would this mean for a student who is _____?*

Step 4: Reflect

- Ahhhhh. I already do this. _____.

- AH HA! This is a new idea. _____.

- HMMMMM. I'm not so sure about _____.

Meghan remembers all too well one example of feedback from her early years of teaching. Her students would complete a math problem-of-the-week, including a written explanation of their problem-solving process. She was committed to giving a numerical evaluation but also personalized written feedback and coaching for each student. Yet despite her good intentions, she found that the extensive written feedback on each submission was time-consuming and meant she was playing catch-up with a backlog of assignments during long weekends and holiday breaks. Additionally, as she reached the end of the stack, the feedback she provided became rushed and less comprehensive.

She acknowledges that there are many things she would do differently today, perhaps with the assignment itself and the emphasis she put on lengthy written feedback, but also in the timeliness and consistency of the feedback she provided. There are also ways Meghan can now reimagine this experience with the use of AI. For instance, she envisions using AI to write a few levels of exemplar responses she could use against student responses, to look for and highlight specific elements in student responses, or even to ask for a list of next steps for the entire class after using an AI tool to do a meta-analysis of all student responses.

## Task Takeover

### Artificial Intelligence and Feedback

Think about how AI can help with feedback. Choose a few examples from the Stop and Jot task that appeared earlier in this chapter, and do some reimagining, keeping in mind the difference between *doing* and *helping*. Though AI can certainly do the task for you, as we have noted it cannot replace the teacher's voice and expertise. Instead, think about ways AI might serve as your helpful assistant as you approach this important but time-consuming aspect of the job. We've added an example to help you get started.

| Teacher-to-Student Feedback | Ways AI Can Support |
| --- | --- |
| Our Example: Giving students feedback on thesis statements submitted for a literary analysis | Have students submit thesis statements electronically and ask AI to sort responses by similarities. Give individualized feedback to the group of like-responses. |
| Your Example: | |
| Your Example: | |

Though feedback is a part of all educators' jobs, it probably looks different for everyone. What you teach, who you teach, and where you teach will change how and when you give feedback. Consider some of these questions as you engage in this Educator Function.

- What do you give feedback on?

- When are you giving feedback?

- What examples of feedback would you like to reimagine?

There are several models that provide a structure for the feedback. We remember the hamburger model, with the top bun being a positive comments, the stuff inside the constructive feedback, and the bottom bun returning to positive comments. Not very sophisticated, we know. And in the hamburger model, the meat of the feedback is left to chance. One study of high school English teachers' written feedback on essays found that while the teachers said they valued highlighting student strengths, 91.4 percent of their written feedback came in the form of error correction (Lee, 2009).

As Panadero and Lipnevich (2021) note, there are at least fourteen feedback models in the published literature. In general, these models each include feedback on content, function, presentation, and source. Each of these factors vary in the different models but there is the recognition that the message is important, that the feedback needs to be used or implemented, that context and relationships matter, and that there are different agents involved in the feedback (those delivering or receiving the feedback).

We will highlight one model for structuring feedback. Then we will turn our attention to the ways in which AI can help with the content of the feedback. Of course, computerized systems can provide feedback and students can seek feedback from others, including AI systems. For now, we focus on a framework that involves students and teachers and a structure for providing feedback.

The GREAT model of feedback was developed by LarkApps, a team productivity and engagement company that specializes in supporting businesses whose employees work remotely but collaborate regularly. They note that empathetic feedback is key to high performance—which is exactly what we all want for our students. The GREAT feedback framework consists of five facets:

- *Growth-oriented*: It signals the intention as constructive and focused on improvement.

- *Real*: It contains honest rather than false praise; it is also targeted—not holistic or vague.

- *Empathetic*: It combines criticism with care and a quest for understanding.

- *Asked-for*: It encourages the receiver to ask questions and seek feedback.

- *Timely*: Since feedback gets stale fast, it is delivered promptly.

## Self-Assessment

*Use the scale to assess your use of various aspects of the GREAT feedback model. What areas do you want to strengthen? How might AI help?*

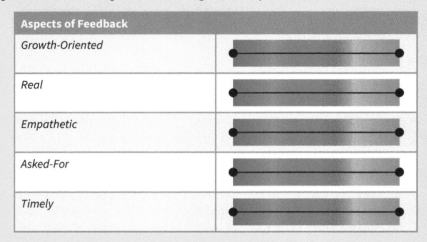

| Aspects of Feedback | |
| --- | --- |
| Growth-Oriented | |
| Real | |
| Empathetic | |
| Asked-For | |
| Timely | |

## USING AI FOR FEEDBACK

There are many ways teachers give students feedback. The choice of feedback style often depends on factors such as the nature of the assignment, subject, or grade level. Furthermore, schools, districts, and teachers have their own norms around giving student feedback.

In one Chicago-area school, a common practice across all grade levels involves providing students with a set of "glow and grow" comments on assignments. Teachers and students embrace this feedback style, which involves always naming one thing done well and one next step. Walking the hallways, visitors might see a "glow and grow" on student artwork, writing samples, and projects. In another school, they focus on peer feedback, and teachers share QR codes on the bottom of student work that link to a video of a peer saying something positive about a classmate's posted work.

Teachers can also utilize AI technology to enhance their existing feedback practices to build upon what is effective rather than to overhaul them entirely. Whether educators are seeking to augment the practice of giving students feedback during one-on-one conferring, providing exemplars to match work against, or giving students comments on a Google doc, there are ways AI can assist.

## PREPARING FOR STUDENT CONFERENCES

Live one-on-one feedback sessions are not unique to education. It is common practice in many industries for employees at all levels to have one-on-one meetings with a supervisor to find out what they are doing well and where they need to go next.

Examples include a team member getting a year-end review from their manager and a CEO getting feedback from a business's board chair. Most teachers are also used to their own one-on-one conferences following an observation or evaluation. This type of feedback is a trusted and effective method that teachers also use in the classroom to work with individual student learners.

Student conferences are focused conversations in which a teacher provides targeted and specific feedback to an individual learner. Using conferring as a teaching method not only fosters opportunities for meaningful connections but also serves as a platform to empower and motivate learners (Shrum, 2019). Allocating time for individual conferences, especially when time is limited, compels us to ensure that each conference is beneficial.

Preparing for a conference requires that we have already reviewed the student work and drafted some feedback. If we have not found time to do so, we might find ourselves either blindly trying to guide students or being tempted to skip the session altogether. With AI, teachers now have access to tools that can assist them in quick conference preparation, even in the minutes that lead up to the one-on-one meeting with a student.

Many of the teacher-facing tools you have explored in previous chapters also have features that can help teachers in giving specific feedback on student work. They have tools that allow users to enter assignment objectives, success criteria, standards, or even a customized rubric along with a specific sample of student work. After teachers fill the required fields and submit the form, these sites generate feedback aligned with the input provided. Good output requires good input. The specificity of the evaluation criteria and the quality of the responses to the prompts influence the usefulness of the feedback.

Briskteaching.com is another tool teachers can use for assistance with feedback, but it does require a paid subscription. One teacher, Melanie, showed us how she uses this AI-aligned Google extension with students she tutors in writing to give feedback right on the Google Doc students are using. She is even able to select the students' grade level and standards, in addition to having the option of adding a list of success criteria that was a part of the assignment. These features ensure that the suggestions the AI provides are as helpful as possible. Of course, Melanie also reviews the feedback it suggests and makes any changes to the content, clarity, and voice where necessary.

Here's another example. Meghan drafted feedback on second-grader Olivia's writing without Brisk, and it looked like this:

On May 12th, 2020 it was Kit's 7th Birthday. On her Birthday, her Grandma got her a pair of roller skates. Kit was so excited to try them out! The next day, Kit's big sister Jill took her to the park so Kit could try out her new roller skates. When they got to the park Kit found the perfect palace to roller skate while Jill got them hot dogs. Then, Jill sat on the bench to watch Kit roller skate. At first, Kit thought it was hard and skinned her knee so she took a break at the bench to have hot dogs with Jill. Now that she was energised, she would be ready to try again! This time Jill held Kit's hand as she rode down the sidewalk. She was actually doing it! Now every day the sisters go to the park to roller skate!

 **Meghan Hargrave**
9 Jul 2020

Olivia, I love how specific you were to think of a character and even a date. The backstory of why she got the roller skates really adds to

Show more

Source: ChatGPT.

Meghan wanted to compare her feedback with feedback on the same writing submission using Brisk. She guided the system to give feedback on a specific standard (third-grade writing standard 3, from the Common Core State Standards). Note that the feedback is organized into major messages with recommendations for next steps.

**Use dialogue to develop experiences and events**

> Next Steps: Consider adding some dialogue to your story to make it more engaging. For example, you could include a conversation between Kit and Jill when they are at the park. This would help to develop their relationship and show their excitement about the roller skates.

**Show the response of characters to situations**

> Next Steps: Instead of just stating that Kit was excited to try out her new roller skates, show her excitement through her actions and thoughts. For example, you could describe how she couldn't stop smiling and bouncing up and down when she saw the roller skates. This would help the reader to understand Kit's response to receiving the gift.

Source: ChatGPT.

Using an AI site dedicated to teaching and learning is one option to expand your feedback, as is visiting an OpenAI site and prompting the chatbot to provide feedback tailored to your needs and style. You may find that the first time you use one of these sites for feedback, you are tempted to copy and paste a body of work and use the most obvious prompt: *Please provide some feedback*. However, unless you provide the chatbot with additional direction, you may find that the feedback is too long and less helpful than you want it to be. It should be no surprise at this point to see that to maximize the effectiveness of AI as a feedback assistant, specific prompting is essential. Keep a log of helpful prompts so that the next time you want help with feedback on student writing, you are ready to go.

Below we share a progression of prompts we used with OpenAI to help with feedback on a piece of student work. Ultimately, the last prompt gave us material that we could use in a one-on-one conference with the student that day.

Prompt #1:

 **You**
Please give feedback on this writing?

In Northern Minnesota, water skiing is a popular sport for people of all ages. Thomas O'Grady, who is almost 9 years old, tried water skiing for the first time during his vacation in Nisswa, Minnesota. This happened on July 4, 2021, at Gull Lake.

Thomas had to make two "almost" attempts before he successfully stood up on two skis. His family, including his mom, dad, brothers, and aunt, cheered him on from the boat. It took three tries, but with his mom's guidance and his dad driving the boat, he made it. Balancing on the skis while the waves moved beneath him was a challenge.

Thomas learned to be patient and persistent, qualities that helped him succeed. His mom, Erin, gave him advice like "bend your knees" and "keep your arms straight" to help him stay balanced on the unpredictable water surface.

Water skiing is a favorite pastime in Minnesota's "lake country," and many people, including Thomas and his two brothers, enjoy this exciting sport.

Source: ChatGPT.

Response:

 **ChatGPT**
Your writing is vivid and engaging, capturing a charming moment of Thomas O'Grady's first experience with water skiing. Here are some positive aspects and suggestions for improvement:

**Positive Aspects:**

1. **Clear and Descriptive:** Your writing provides a clear picture of the setting, the individuals involved, and the challenges faced by Thomas. This makes it easy for the reader to visualize the scene.
2. **Emotional Connection:** By mentioning the family cheering for Thomas, you create an emotional connection that adds warmth to the story. It's evident that this experience was a shared and celebrated moment.
3. **Chronological Order:** The events are presented in a logical sequence, starting with the introduction of the sport, Thomas's attempts, and the eventual success. This chronological order helps in following the narrative smoothly.
4. **Relevant Details:** The inclusion of specific details such as the location (Nisswa, Minnesota), the date (July 4, 2021), and the lake (Gull Lake) enhances the authenticity and completeness of the narrative.

↓

**Suggestions for Improvement:**

1. **Show, Don't Tell:** While you describe the events well, consider incorporating more sensory details to make the experience even more vivid. For example, describe the feel of the wind, the sound of the boat engine, or the taste of the lake air. This helps readers immerse themselves in the scene.
2. **Expand on Emotions:** Delve a bit deeper into Thomas's emotions during the attempts. Was he nervous, excited, or determined? Exploring his emotional journey can add another layer to the story.
3. **Vary Sentence Structure:** Introduce some sentence variety to enhance the flow and rhythm of the narrative. Mix short and long sentences to create a dynamic and engaging reading experience.
4. **Conclusion or Reflection:** Consider adding a concluding sentence or a reflection on the significance of this experience for Thomas. How did this achievement impact him? Did it leave a lasting impression?

---

Source: ChatGPT.

Prompt #2:

 **You**
This is a piece of 5th grade information writing. The assignment was to write a news article about a true event. Please name three things the writer work next.

In Northern Minnesota, water skiing is a popular sport for people of all ages. Thomas O'Grady, who is almost 9 years old, tried water skiing for the first time during his vacation in Nisswa, Minnesota. This happened on July 4, 2021, at Gull Lake.

Thomas had to make two "almost" attempts before he successfully stood up on two skis. His family, including his mom, dad, brothers, and aunt, cheered him on from the boat. It took three tries, but with his mom's guidance and his dad driving the boat, he made it. Balancing on the skis while the waves moved beneath him was a challenge.

Thomas learned to be patient and persistent, qualities that helped him succeed. His mom, Erin, gave him advice like "bend your knees" and "keep your arms straight" to help him stay balanced on the unpredictable water surface.

Water skiing is a favorite pastime in Minnesota's "lake country," and many people, including Thomas and his two brothers, enjoy this exciting sport.

---

Source: ChatGPT.

Response:

 **ChatGPT**
**Three Areas for Improvement:**

1. **Include Direct Quotes:**
   * Encourage the writer to include direct quotes from Thomas or his family members. This can add a personal touch to the article and make it more engaging for readers. For example, including a quote from Thomas about how he felt during his first successful attempt or a comment from his mom on the importance of patience and persistence.

2. **Enhance Descriptive Language:**
   * Suggest incorporating more descriptive language to create a vivid picture of the scene. For instance, the writer can describe the sound of the boat engine, the feeling of the wind, or the excitement in the air. Adding sensory details will make the article more immersive for the readers.

3. **Expand on the Conclusion:**
   * Encourage the writer to expand on the conclusion by providing a reflection on the significance of Thomas's achievement. How did this experience impact him, and what did he learn from it? A thoughtful reflection can add depth to the article and provide a satisfying conclusion for the readers.

Source: ChatGPT.

Prompt #3:

 **You**
This 5th grader was assigned to write an informational piece of writing that was a news brief about a true event. Please give feedback on the writing naming one thing they were successful at and one thing they could work on. Follow the format for feedback below and address the writer directly in the comments.

Success:

Area for Growth:

This is a piece of 5th grade information writing. The assignment was to write a news article about a true event. Please name three things the writer work next.

In Northern Minnesota, water skiing is a popular sport for people of all ages. Thomas O'Grady, who is almost 9 years old, tried water skiing for the first time during his vacation in Nisswa, Minnesota. This happened on July 4, 2021, at Gull Lake.

Thomas had to make two "almost" attempts before he successfully stood up on two skis. His family, including his mom, dad, brothers, and aunt, cheered him on from the boat. It took three tries, but with his mom's guidance and his dad driving the boat, he made it. Balancing on the skis while the waves moved beneath him was a challenge.

Thomas learned to be patient and persistent, qualities that helped him succeed. His mom, Erin, gave him advice like "bend your knees" and "keep your arms straight" to help him stay balanced on the unpredictable water surface.

Water skiing is a favorite pastime in Minnesota's "lake country," and many people, including Thomas and his two brothers, enjoy this exciting sport.

Source: ChatGPT.

Response:

 **ChatGPT**

**Success:**

Great job, Writer! You successfully convey the key details of Thomas O'Grady's wate
skiing experience in a clear and engaging manner. The news brief effectively captur
the excitement of the moment, providing a vivid picture of Thomas's perseverance a
eventual success.

**Area for Growth:**

As you continue to develop your writing, consider adding more descriptive details t(
make the story even more captivating. Think about incorporating sensory elements
such as the sound of the boat, the feeling of the wind, or the cheers from the family.
This will help your readers to feel more immersed in the experience and make your
news brief even more compelling. Keep up the excellent work!

Source: ChatGPT.

## Try It Out!

### Preparing for Student Conferences

To engage in this component, you will need writing that you can copy and paste into an OpenAI site. This could be student work you have accessible or even a sample of something you wrote.

Step 1: Visit your favorite OpenAI chatbot.

Step 2: Give the prompt *Give me feedback on this writing*, followed by the writing itself.

Step 3: Study the results with the following questions in mind.

- Is this feedback helpful?
- Would a student in my class be able to use this feedback effectively?
- Does the feedback offer productive coaching on the piece?

Step 4: Revise the prompt to give context to the assignment.

- Describe the work you are sharing.
- Provide information about the student.
- Identify the task or what are they trying to do.
- Name the standards being taught.

Step 5: Study results with the following questions in mind.

- How are the results different?
- Is this feedback helpful? Which is more helpful?
- Would a student in my class be able to use this feedback effectively?
- Does the feedback offer productive coaching on the piece?

Step 6: Revise the prompt to include the format of output.

- How much feedback should the AI tool provide?
- What is the ideal format for the feedback?
- What should I call the feedback it gives?

Step 7: Study results with the following questions in mind.

- What additional insights did you gain?
- Is this feedback helpful? How so?
- Would a student in my class be able to use this feedback effectively?
- Does the feedback offer productive coaching on the piece?

Step 8: Reflect. What does this teach you about prompting for feedback on student work? What will you include in future AI prompts when seeking student feedback? What else do you want to try?

## STUDENT EXEMPLAR RESPONSES

Exemplars, which are specific examples of student work, are a familiar tool in most classrooms. Exemplars are carefully selected examples that educators and students use as concrete representations of standards and objectives in action (Hawe et al., 2021). Exemplars can help reduce the subjectivity associated with human feedback, and they can serve as a guide for determining some of the feedback that teachers can provide on student work. By establishing agreed-upon exemplars, teachers and students can see standards in action and have a set benchmark for what student responses can and should look like.

For example, a group of third-grade teachers were preparing to teach a literary essay unit for the first time. Together they outlined the learning progression, the essential skills to teach, and success criteria for student writing. As they prepared, they found themselves wondering what student work would look like. They considered what learning third graders realistically needed to work toward in a literary essay, and what teachers should be looking for when reviewing student work throughout the unit. They decided to use an AI tool to help them get started in creating exemplars that represented a range of skills and needs to share when teaching the unit.

Using a teacher-facing AI site, the third-grade teachers created a prompt that gave them a starting point for useful examples. Entering the grade level, standard, length, success criteria, and assignment produced an example that was a close fit to what they were looking for. Additionally, this tool gave them a nonexample and even an option to expand on the prompt with additional text evidence. Finally, they were able to take these responses to create three levels of exemplars, including samples that demonstrate the following:

- Beginning levels of proficiency with grade-level standards
- Developing levels of proficiency with grade-level standards
- Proficiency in meeting standards

These teachers used MagicSchool.ai because it is useful for exemplars and nonexemplars, but this could also be done with an Open AI tool. Also, the Exemplar & Non-exemplar feature on Aiforeducation.com provides similar results.

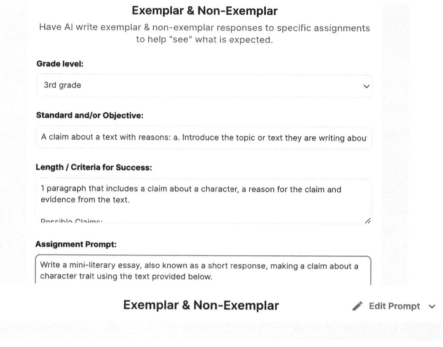

**Exemplar & Non-Exemplar**

Have AI write exemplar & non-exemplar responses to specific assignments to help "see" what is expected.

**Grade level:**

> 3rd grade                                                                                 ⌄

**Standard and/or Objective:**

> A claim about a text with reasons: a. Introduce the topic or text they are writing abou

**Length / Criteria for Success:**

> 1 paragraph that includes a claim about a character, a reason for the claim and evidence from the text.
>
> Possible Claims:

**Assignment Prompt:**

> Write a mini-literary essay, also known as a short response, making a claim about a character trait using the text provided below.

**Exemplar & Non-Exemplar**                                           ✏ Edit Prompt ⌄

**Exemplary Response:**

The tree is a good friend because she always supports and cares for the boy. Throughout the text, the tree is always there for the boy, offering him shade to sleep, apples to eat, and branches to play on. She even suggests that the boy sell her apples to get money when he expresses his desire for it. The tree's selflessness and willingness to give up her own resources demonstrate her loyalty and kindness as a friend.

**Non-Exemplary Response:**

The tree is good because it gives the boy things. The tree offers the boy apples, branches, and trunk to fulfill his wishes. The boy wants money, a house, and a boat, and the tree gives them to him. This shows that the tree is good because it gives the boy what he wants.

👍 👎

Can you add more examples of how the tree is a good friend?

Certainly! Here are a few more examples of how the tree is a good friend:

1. The tree provides a safe and comfortable place for the boy to rest. In the text, it says, "And when he was tired, he would sleep in her shade." This shows that the tree offers a peaceful spot for the boy to relax and rejuvenate.
2. The tree encourages the boy to be happy and enjoy himself. It states, "Come, Boy, come and climb up my trunk and swing from my branches and be happy." The tree actively invites the boy to have fun and experience joy in its presence.
3. The tree sacrifices its own resources to fulfill the boy's desires. When the boy asks for money, a house, and a boat, the tree offers its apples, branches, and trunk respectively. This demonstrates the tree's willingness to give up its own possessions for the boy's happiness.

These examples further emphasize the tree's role as a good friend, showcasing its support, encouragement, and selflessness towards the boy.

👍 👎

| Version | Essay |
|---------|-------|
| Version 1 | The tree and the boy had a good friendship. The tree provided comfort and support, as shown in the text when the boy slept in her shade and she invited him to rest. This means the tree was a good friend. |
| Version 2 (Exemplar) | The tree is a good friend. The tree is a good friend because she always provides comfort and support to the boy. In the text it said, "And when he was tired, he would sleep in her shade," and "Come, Boy, sit down. Sit down and rest." These examples show that the tree cared about the boy and how the boy felt which means that the tree was a good friend. |
| Version 3 | In the book The Giving Tree by Shel Silverstein, the tree is a good friend. The tree is a good friend because she always provides comfort and support to the boy. In the text it says, "And when he was tired, he would sleep in her shade," and "Come boy, sit down. Sit down and rest." Another time that the tree is a good friend is when she plays games with the boy. The text says, "Come, Boy, come and climb up my trunk and swing from my branches and be happy." These are both examples show that the tree cared about the boy, when the boy wanted to relax he let him relax and when he wanted to play he let him play. The way the tree cares about the boy shows that she is a very good friend. |

## Try It Out!

## Creating Student Exemplars

Take time to explore the ways AI can help create different work exemplars. You might engage in this component with colleagues as you plan a unit, analyze standards, or look closely at student work.

Step 1: Visit the teacher-facing AI site www.magicschool.ai.

Step 2: Select the Magic Tool: "Exemplar & Nonexemplar."

Step 3: Fill in necessary information in the boxes provided: Grade Level, Standard and/or Objective, Length/Criteria for Success, and Assignment Prompt.

Step 4: Generate.

Step 5: Review output for content, clarity, and voice.

Step 6: Revise as necessary.

## Prompt Writing Tips

- Use the same information in Step 3 when writing an original prompt on an LLM site like ChatGPT.

- If appropriate, include multiple standards and objectives where prompted.

- Include any expectations you have for the assignment in your prompt or in the boxes provided. This might include format, required components, or even content to avoid.

## SELF- AND PEER FEEDBACK

For decades, educators have been overwhelmed by the volume of student work submitted, and most teachers feel pressure to look at it all. To improve the efficiency of the task, we encourage teachers to have students reflect on or highlight certain aspects of their work to give a more targeted starting point for the teacher. We also encourage teachers to have students self-assess their work and use that as feedback for improvement. Further, educators can teach students to provide feedback to peers, because there are far more peers than there are teachers in a given classroom. Having said that, we also recognize that students need support to obtain feedback from and provide it to peers.

When an athlete is practicing, having a coach on the sidelines giving cues and encouragement directly impacts performance. Teachers try their best to be the coach to students, but this is not always possible. However, with the advent of AI tools, students can receive real-time feedback in new ways.

It is important to teach students how to use AI to get productive feedback that is targeted, specific, actionable, and tailored to their needs. Teachers should model for students how to get this type of feedback from AI and how to use the feedback to make revisions. Here are some useful points to share as you model:

- Create writing prompts that include specific details for the feedback requested. For example, if writers want feedback on their use of commas or overall sentence structure, they can use the prompt *Please give me feedback on the use of commas and overall sentence structure for the writing below.*

- Include the success criteria the writer is working on when asking the tool for feedback.

- Ask for help with specific parts of the work. Avoid copying and pasting lengthy pieces of work. Instead, work on one part at a time.

- Focus on places where the writer is unsure of the work and wants a second opinion. Instead of asking the teacher, "Is this okay?" or "Is this right?" writers can use AI by entering the work they are unsure of and then getting feedback that can either confirm that the writer is on the right track or give a next step.

## Classroom Connections

### Peer Feedback

Engaging students in peer feedback provides students with an opportunity to have eyes on more examples. This approach also builds community and supports learning. This is probably why so many state standards include some sort of peer learning or peer feedback. This process looks different depending on the subject area and the age of the students, but in each case it requires that the student who is giving the feedback must look critically at another student's work and respond. Though this response comes with good intention, teachers report that students sometimes struggle to give meaningful feedback that will actually coach a peer into next steps.

Just as teachers can request feedback from AI, so can students. Showing students how to use generative AI to prepare to give a peer feedback is a helpful skill. In particular, modeling and teaching students how to turn existing peer feedback prompts into AI prompts is a powerful exercise (see Table 8).

**Table 8** • Peer Feedback Supported by AI

| Ways Peers Give Feedback | Prompts for AI Assistance |
|---|---|
| Cheerlead | Name three things this student is good at. |
| | What makes this part so funny/entertaining/good? |
| Listen | What is one section that needs clarification? |
| | Who would be the audience for this work? |
| | What are a few questions I can ask about this work? |
| Teach | What are two tips I could give to make the work below better? |
| | What would make this assignment better? |
| | Give two things this person could do next. |
| Coach | What should they keep doing? |
| | What are things they should try again? |
| | Give three reminders or tips. |

As you teach students to use AI tools in this way, you can also emphasize the importance of rereading, analyzing, and revising the content generated. Explain that AI can offer assistance, but it requires a human to be in the loop. This skill and lesson will take time, and it will require modeling and explicit teaching throughout the year. Student users will likely improve with each opportunity.

When students use AI in this manner, be on the lookout for skills you can address in future lessons. Use these occasions as opportunities to coach students toward the productive use of tools they will have access to in years to come.

## Check for Understanding

We used AI to help generate discussion questions to assist you and your colleagues as you think more about the role of AI in classroom feedback. Check for understanding of content in the Educator Function by writing thoughts about each question or using them to guide an in-person discussion with other teachers. (See Appendix for answers to all Check for Understanding questions.)

*(Continued)*

(Continued)

Discussion Question 1: How can AI tools be used to enhance the quality and quantity of actionable feedback that students receive in the classroom?

Discussion Question 2: What are the potential benefits and limitations of using AI for providing feedback to students, especially in relation to the timeliness and specificity of the feedback?

Discussion Questions 3: How might the integration of AI tools in feedback processes influence students' ability to seek and utilize feedback effectively, and what implications does this have for their learning journey and growth mindset?

## CONCLUSION

We all appreciate feedback that is useful (not critical); it helps us accomplish a goal or improve our practice. For teachers, providing feedback can be a challenge, particularly given the range of learners that exists in the classroom and the fixed amount of time we have for teaching, learning, and assessing. Feedback content can be easily generated by AI, reducing the amount of time educators spend identifying what to share with students. All it takes is clear criteria and knowing what students are supposed to be learning.

# Educator Function #6

## Lifelong Learning

**EDUCATOR FUNCTION CHALLENGE**

- Continue learning throughout your career and use AI as a support system and thought partner.

Lifelong learning is a necessary function and is important when embracing life's next steps, adapting to societal changes, and acquiring the essential skills and tools needed to actively engage in new activities and experiences. According to a 2023 *Forbes* article, lifelong learning "is a continuous process that helps individuals stay relevant in their fields, keep up with changes in trends and adapt to ambiguity" (McGrath, 2023). Many industries require ongoing professional learning to ensure that employees remain current on best practices, prevailing research, and advancements within their respective fields. For example, a physician is expected to provide care that is as current as possible. Similarly, professional learning is an important function of our work as educators, and we have engaged in countless workshops and conferences in our lives.

As we guide students to learn new skills and expand content knowledge, we also respond to the students' curiosity, inquiries, and wonderings. In addition to staying current in content knowledge, educators must also stay up to date with evolving and evidence-based teaching practices and instructional methods; teachers at all levels share the obligation to stay on top of developments in the field (Serviss, 2022). Consequently, a willingness to be a lifelong learner is essential for teaching, whether we are a first-year teacher or we have been teaching for many years.

115

**Stop and Jot**

Take some time to think about some of the skills you have had to learn in your current role. Consider content and methods. What new content have you had to learn? What new teaching techniques and methods have you incorporated in your practice? Jot some ideas in the chart below.

| New Content (Academic Topics and Current Events) | Teaching Practices (Instructional Techniques and Methods) |
|---|---|
|  |  |
|  |  |
|  |  |
|  |  |

**Ask a Bot**

Take time to think about ways AI can be used to support lifelong learning. Using the steps provided here, engage in a back-and-forth conversation to consider ways AI can help you stay current on academic topics or current events. How can it help you learn about teaching practices, including instructional techniques and methods?

Step 1. Sign in to your favorite chatbot.

Step 2. Ask the chatbot these guiding questions about how it can support lifelong learning.

- *How can AI help me be a lifelong learner?*
- *How can AI help me learn about new content better than a Google search?*
- *Give a few prompts to use with chatbots to stay updated on current events.*
- *Can AI help teach new teaching methods?*
- *What are some teaching techniques I should learn about _____?*

Step 3. Engage in a conversation with the chatbot using the *change* or *add-on* prompts below.

- *Can you give me an example?*

- *Consolidate the response into one big idea.*

- *Please explain _____.*

- *What else should I keep in mind?*

- *What else should I know about this?*

- *Are there other things to consider?*

- *What about _____?*

Step 4. Reflect

- Ahhhhh. I already do this _____.

- AH HA! This is a new idea. _____.

- HMMMMM. I'm not so sure about _____.

Artificial Intelligence tools not only can be a valuable support in helping teachers acquire the information needed to stay current, but also can serve as a resource for processing and making sense of information. There are instances in which we encounter compelling ideas at a professional learning session or while reading a professional book like this one. Often these ideas seem interesting and appear to have the potential to make a difference in our teaching, but they may not apply or fit exactly as they are presented. For instance, maybe the idea was accompanied with an example for another grade level or content area. Or maybe the technique will not quite fit with the structures already in place in our classroom. When time permits, as with many of the other educator functions we have covered, we can collaborate with colleagues, a mentor, or an instructional coach about how to make these ideas our own. We can also look to AI, since it has shown the ability to be a helpful assistant in this area.

**Try It Out!**

Exploring an Idea

Step 1: Revisit one of the Educator Functions in this book, looking for an idea you came across that seemed to have potential but wasn't specific to your content or grade level.

Step 2: Visit your favorite chatbot.

Step 3: Write a prompt with the assistance of one of the templates below.

*(Continued)*

(Continued)

- *I read that _____ can help _____ do _____. As a _____-grade teacher, I am trying to think about how this could help me. What ideas do you have for how this suggestion could work in my classroom?*

- *Here is a suggestion for how AI can support teachers with the function of _____. I teach _____ to _____ grade. Give examples and ideas specific to my grade-level and content area.*

- *_____ teachers are using AI to help them _____. I am a _____-grade teacher. How can AI help me in the same way?*

- Create your own!

Step 4: Look carefully at the output, and engage in more conversation if necessary, using or modifying some of the suggestions below.

- *Can you give me an example?*

- *This is a great idea, but it will not work because of _____. Please adjust accordingly.*

- *What else?*

- *Also keep in mind _____ and _____.*

- *What would this look like when students are learning about _____?*

## Self-Assessment

The U.S. Department of Education's Office of Educational Technology developed the following professional learning self-assessment tool, which focuses on online and blended learning opportunities for teachers (U.S. Department of Education, 2017). Consider each of these characteristics of high-quality and evidence-based professional learning strategies as they apply to your learning. Then identify some of the ways that AI could help you with each of these.

| Qualities of Professional Learning | |
| --- | --- |
| Promotes self-directed learning through active participation in online spaces | |
| Involves participants in online communities of practice that support innovation for improved learning | |
| Models use of technology to explore real-world issues | |
| Advances the use of technology for sharing practice (e.g., posting a lesson plan for peer review) | |
| Supports collaborative knowledge construction via various communication and collaboration tools | |

| Qualities of Professional Learning | |
|---|---|
| Encourages the customization and personalization of learning activities through the use of digital tools and resources | |
| Supports technology use to facilitate a variety of effective assessment and evaluation strategies | |
| Involves the use of social media in instructionally sound ways that benefit and amplify learning | |
| Makes effective use of current and emerging digital tools to support research | |
| Models and teaches safe, legal, and ethical use of digital information and technology | |
| Focuses on strategies that require equitable access to appropriate digital tools and resources for all | |
| Uses digital-age communication and collaboration tools to extend cultural understanding and global awareness | |

*Source*: Professional learning strategies self-assessment tool. Retrieved from https://tech.ed.gov/wp-content/uploads/2014/11/Section-3-Strategies-Self-Assessment-FINAL.pdf

## CLARIFYING OR REFRESHING CONTENT KNOWLEDGE

Changing grade levels or taking on a new content area creates an obvious need for additional learning, but even teachers who are in the same grade-level or content area for many years should be learning new content across their career. Sometimes even revisiting material you have not taught for a year requires a little bit of a brush-up. Of course, doing a Google search or flipping through curricular resources can help, but AI provides the opportunity for you to engage in a much more in-depth and personalized experience.

A group of veteran middle school teachers in Connecticut were teaching from a new textbook. The textbook suggested they address motifs during a unit focused on finding themes within a text. The group was not sure what this meant, and their quick Google search didn't provide much support or definition. Consequently, one teacher simply noted their question, and then they waited until they had time with a staff developer a few weeks later to understand what this meant and how they should explain it to students.

With AI, teachers in a similar situation might not need to wait. Instead of typing one question into Google and receiving a single answer, teachers can engage in dynamic conversations with a chatbot. In our example, the chatbot would not only define the term *motif* as it applies to their content, it would also delve into further thinking when engaging with a chain of prompts like *Provide an example that would resonate with an eighth grader* or *How should I approach teaching this to my students?* or even *Explain why students should know this and how it will help them better understand the theme.*

Interacting with a chatbot in this way has the capability of facilitating human-like dialogue, helping users build knowledge and understanding that is tailored to their specific needs. Engaging in conversational prompt chains with general AI platforms like ChatGPT or Bard enables users to interact in a dynamic conversation, surpassing the static nature of a traditional online search engine.

## Try It Out!

### Clarifying Content or Concepts

Step 1: Name a topic or concept you would like to know more about.

Step 2: Visit your favorite chatbot.

Step 3: Ask the chatbot to teach you about the topic using one of these prompts.

- *What is _____?*
- *What does _____ mean for _____ graders?*
- *Can you tell me _____ things I need to know about _____ as a teacher?*
- *Explain _____ to help me understand _____.*

Step 4: Engage in at least four prompt chains. You can use these follow-up questions and prompts or your own.

- *Explain more about _____.*
- *Tell me more about _____.*
- *Can you give me an example?*
- *I don't understand _____. Can you break it down for me?*
- *Are there examples of _____ you suggest I share with my students?*
- *What would this mean for _____-grade curriculum?*
- *Can you give me suggestions for how to teach _____?*

Step 5: Reflect on what you learned.

Step 6: Continue asking more questions, focusing on gaining confidence and clarity in this area. As you do this, think about how this use of AI is similar to having a mentor by your side.

## Classroom Connection

### Learning Refresher

Teachers are not the only ones who might need a little refresher on content. Students are asked to hold onto a lot of learning from year to year and class to class. Teach students to engage in effective and thoughtful conversation with AI to remind them of content they have learned before and help them tap into prior knowledge using some of the question stems below. Students can engage in a back-and-forth with an OpenAI chatbot or engage in an assigned conversation to refresh their learning with student-facing discussion sites like Socrat.ai and Parlay.ai.

Topic Introduction

- What is _____?
- What are the most important things to know about _____?

Deeper Understanding

- Can you explain why _____ is important for _____?
- How does _____ relate to _____?

Context

- What is the history of _____?
- What does _____ have to do with _____?
- What background knowledge is helpful when studying _____?

## RETHINKING INSTRUCTION

Educators are constantly making decisions. In fact, research indicates that teachers make up to 1,500 decisions in a given day, and some educators actually believe this number is low (Klein, 2021). Each year, each unit, each day, teachers rethink assignments and learning experiences to fit within a specific amount of time and for a certain group of students. Making these decisions is time-consuming and exhausting, and the process often requires that teachers learn a new approach or idea to make the learning fit. AI tools can also help ease some of this cognitive load.

As a group of fourth-grade teachers in Poughkeepsie, New York, were implementing a new math curriculum, they were required to adhere to a districtwide pacing guide. However, some students needed extra time to practice fact fluency. In the past, the teachers had dedicated fifteen minutes every day to fact fluency, but under the new requirements, they lost the dedicated time to build this foundational math skill. After the first assessment, they knew something had to change, but they could not conceptualize how they could fit a fifteen-minute practice into such a tight timeline. They decided to turn to AI for help.

They engaged with ChatGPT by using the following prompt:

*Do you have an idea for how to help my fourth graders with fact fluency? We only have, at most, five minutes a day to dedicate to this activity. Can you suggest something that is replicable, low prep, and effective?*

The bot replied with several ideas and ultimately helped them identify an approach for this important skill. From the options provided, the teachers decided to implement stations in which students engaged in one-minute rotations. At each station, students would practice facts before moving to the next. These educators learned that creating a daily challenge not only was an easy way to include fact fluency but also helped students track and monitor their own progress.

This new learning reenergized the group of teachers. They agreed that they would use AI tools again the next time they needed to learn a new way of approaching a challenge in the classroom.

## ✎ Stop and Jot

Reflect and make a list of practices and content you are struggling to find time to include in your classroom. You might think about skills students need more practice with, lessons you have taught in past years, or even teaching structures you want to fit in but are not sure how. Then complete the following chart:

| Teaching Considerations | Reflect on things you have not had time to include, have had to let go of, or struggle to fit in regularly. |
| --- | --- |
| Lessons or Activities | (e.g., parts of speech, Socratic seminars, poetry unit) |

| Student Skills | (e.g., fact fluency, editing for punctuation, citations) |
|---|---|
| | |
| Teaching Structures | (e.g., small-group teaching, book clubs or literature circles, partnerships) |
| | |

As with all the other functions addressed throughout this playbook, the more details you can provide, the more likely it is that the ideas generated will fit your needs. The fourth-grade teachers described here were seeking to learn about a new way of doing things, and they were sure to include the details about the grade level, purpose of activity, and time available. Consequently, they were not provided with generic ideas; they received suggestions specific to their needs and the needs of their students.

## Task-Takeover

### Learning a New Approach

Let's try a task-takeover to see how AI can help us learn a new approach for managing student partnerships. To begin, open ChatGPT (or another general AI tool) and start a new chat. Type in this prompt:

*(Continued)*

(Continued)

> *I am a teacher who wants my students to get better at working in partnerships.*
> *Right now when they work together, they are usually distracted and off*
> *task. I want to dedicate five minutes three times a week to having students*
> *productively work together to share their work and process what they learned*
> *that day. What ideas do you have that could help?*

When we followed these steps, the bot produced twelve suggestions. Look at the response you receive, and decide which suggestions feel most appropriate for your students. Engage in at least a few more back-and-forth exchanges with the bot. We were impressed with how quickly we learned new ideas using some of these prompts.

- *Can you give me more ideas for _____?*
- *What are some more _____ that I can use to _____?*
- *Keep in mind that I only have _____ minutes.*
- *_____ is a great idea, but adjust it so that _____.*

## TEACHER COACHING AND FEEDBACK

Just as AI tools have proven effective for student feedback, as outlined in Educator Function #4, so to can they be effective in giving teachers feedback on lessons, assignments, materials created, and even teaching itself. One study, aimed at getting a deeper understanding of K–12 teachers' perspectives on feedback, reported that two of the most resounding things teachers want are to get feedback quickly and to get feedback in meaningful, non-threatening ways (Guskey & Link, 2022). Teachers reported that timely feedback makes it more likely that changes or shifts will be made, and getting specific feedback that feels targeted but nonjudgmental proves most beneficial. We have found that AI tools can help with both.

Using open AI sites to get feedback on a lesson plan or student assignment is one simple way to put it to use for this purpose. Perhaps you copy and paste an assignment with the prompt, *How could this assignment better address standard _____?* or, *Give feedback on how explicit the instruction is on _____.* You might also ask for specific suggestions like, *I am trying to work on student engagement. What suggestions do you have for revisions or additions that will help me do that?* We have found that doing this with groups of teacher teams during grade-level meetings or after-school professional learning sessions has led to some incredible Ah Ha moments around the realization that there is a teaching tool that can provide productive and helpful feedback that can make assignments and lessons better.

There are also teacher-facing AI sites that provide feedback on lessons. For example, TeachFX is a platform dedicated to using AI technology to provide teachers with regular, automated feedback. It is essentially an AI-powered instructional coach that can give teachers specific and targeted feedback on instruction, specifically components of instruction like student talk versus teacher talk, levels of questioning, and student response. The TeachFX app voice records a lesson, or conversation, and provides various reports that help teachers, and even students, reflect accordingly. Being able to get real-time data on the use of academic vocabulary, student contributions, explicitness of teacher voice, and amount of think-time provided opens a world of opportunities for teachers' own growth and personalized lifelong learning.

# NEW POSSIBILITIES

The most rewarding aspect of engaging with AI lies in the continuous discovery of new teaching ideas through the simple step of interacting with and using teacher-facing AI platforms. In our own experiences, we noticed right away that there were tools included on these sites that we were not familiar with before. We found that whether it is delving into evidence-based strategies, learning about the science of learning, or really getting to know the concept of choice boards, there are always new things to learn or new explanations of these ideas.

Spending time navigating the wide range of tools offered by platforms like Eduaide.Ai, Socrat.ai, or Magicschool.ai has exposed us to innovative ideas to bring to the classroom. In essence, our exploration of these sites has become our own professional learning session and has left us with new methods and teaching tools applicable in the classroom.

Table 9 outlines some of the tools we have come across on these sites. What do you already know? What do you use? What do you not know and want to learn more about?

**Table 9** • Self-Assessment of Some Tools Available on Educational AI Sites

| Tool or Feature | Know | Use | Don't Know Yet |
|---|---|---|---|
| Jigsaw Activity | | | |
| Evidence-Based Strategies | | | |
| Think-Pair-Share | | | |
| Taxonomy Scaffolding | | | |

*(Continued)*

(Continued)

| Tool or Feature | Know | Use | Don't Know Yet |
|---|---|---|---|
| Evidence Statements | | | |
| Learning Stations | | | |
| Stand Up, Sit Down | | | |
| Quiz, Quiz, Trade | | | |
| DOK Questions | | | |
| Project-Based Learning | | | |
| 5E Model Lesson Plan | | | |
| 3D Science Assessment | | | |
| Restorative Reflection | | | |
| Socratic Dialogue | | | |

## Try It Out!

### Learning New Teaching Techniques

Step 1: Visit one of these AI sites: Socrat.ai, Parlay.ai, Magicschool.ai, or Eduaide.Ai.

Step 2: Identify a tool or feature that is familiar to you but is not one you currently use.

Step 3: Following the prompts provided by the system, create an assignment or activity appropriate for the students you teach.

Step 4: Reflect.

- *Why did you let go of the tool or feature?*
- *Would it be helpful for you to bring it back?*
- *How can the AI tool assist you in this process?*

Step 5: Find a tool or feature that is not familiar to you and that you do not yet use.

Step 6: Start by exploring the tool to build an understanding of what it is and how it can be used for teaching and learning.

Step 7: Following the prompts provided by the system, create an assignment or activity appropriate for the students you teach.

Step 8: Reflect.

- Would this be a helpful tool or feature for your grade-level or content area?
- How can the AI tool assist you in this process?

Step 9: Repeat this approach for other features and tools that you want to explore.

## Check for Understanding

As a final check for understanding, we asked AI to help create some scenario-based questions that will allow you to apply the content covered in this Educator Function. On your own or working with a colleague, read each scenario below and consider how AI can support lifelong learning and how you would respond in this situation using the content of this Educator Function. (See Appendix for answers to all Check for Understanding questions.)

*(Continued)*

(Continued)

*Scenario 1:* You are an educator attending a professional development session where you learn about a new teaching approach. How would you utilize AI tools to further understand and adapt this approach to fit your specific classroom needs and student population?

*Scenario 2:* You are a teacher who needs to clarify a specific topic or concept related to your content area. How would you use AI to engage in a dynamic conversation to gain a deeper understanding tailored to your specific teaching needs?

*Scenario 3:* You're a seasoned educator contemplating adjusting your instructional approach to better align with your students' needs. How might AI serve as a valuable resource in teaching you about new activities or teaching methods you can use with this particular group of learners?

## CONCLUSION

If you have reached this point of the book, you are likely a lifelong learner who is interested in continually honing your craft. You recognize that there is still so much to learn, and you experience a certain level of excitement when you learn new things. By accepting the Educator Function challenge, you are well on your way of developing new knowledge and skills with the help of AI.

# CONCLUSION

As with many technological changes—from the chalkboard in 1830 to the widespread adoption of one-to-one devices in 2020—the integration of artificial intelligence (AI) into education will be both a hot topic and a necessary one for educators at all levels. Teachers, students, leaders, and caregivers/families will continue to familiarize themselves with the capabilities of existing AI technologies and their impact on various aspects of teaching and learning. Simultaneously, learning about, navigating, and embracing new AI tools and platforms that are sure to emerge will continue to challenge us all.

At the close of 2023, *EdWeek* shared the top ten things teachers are looking for in the year(s) to come, and to no surprise, AI made the list (Will, 2023). The report pointed out that expanded access to artificial intelligence poses new challenges and opportunities. It also revealed that almost half of the educators surveyed, including district leaders, principals, and teachers, expressed discomfort with AI technologies they have encountered or anticipate encountering in the very near future. With all the ways AI can and will positively impact the field of education—ways we hope you have come to realize while engaging with this playbook—it is imperative not to let this discomfort keep you from exploring, learning, and embracing this new frontier.

We hope that the possibilities and realities of AI will bring you anything but discomfort, and that this book has left you excited about all it has to offer. For teachers, learning ways AI can engage students, develop content, plan instruction, and think alongside you should bring newfound energy into functions of the job that may currently feel time-consuming, challenging, or overwhelming. As we prepare to conclude this playbook, here are some final recommendations:

- Have fun continuing to explore all that is available.
- Give yourself permission to try new things and adjust accordingly.
- Celebrate the wins.

As you move forward, use the adoption of AI in education as an opportunity to collaborate with and learn alongside your colleagues as you all get to know the capabilities of AI at the same time. For the most part, we are all novices with a tool that is in its infancy, and we can embrace this opportunity to learn together.

In Chapter 1, Getting to Know AI, we introduced you to the Kübler-Ross Change Curve (Figure 3). We hope by experimenting and actively engaging with AI tools in this playbook, you will be ready to progress toward the next phases of the curve, moving toward making informed decisions about which AI tools are most beneficial for you and can be successfully integrated into your daily teaching practice. In fact, the Kübler–Ross model is strikingly similar to another model introduced in 1995 to diagram the patterns that come with each new technological innovation (see Figure 12).

**Figure 12** • The Gartner Hype Cycle

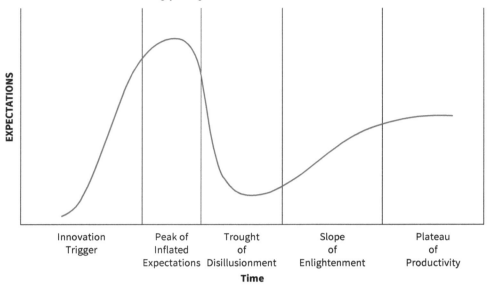

Source: Gartner, Understanding Gartner's Hype Cycles, Philip Dawson, Jan-Martin Lowendahl, Felix Gaehtgens, 24 July 2023. GARTNER and HYPE CYCLE are trademarks of Gartner Inc. and/or its affiliates.

The Gartner Hype Cycle shows how the maturity and adoption of technology generates positive change and productive use for those who engage with it. The model's creators refer to the initial phase of learning a new technology as the technology Innovation Trigger, which is followed by the Peak of Inflated Expectations (Gartner, 2023). You may have found yourself at this peak in the early chapters of this book, perhaps followed by a little bit of disillusionment (the next phase) as you attempted—and will continue to attempt—some things that maybe did not go as planned. However, you start to integrate AI into your daily functions, there will no doubt be instances of enlightenment when the ways it can support and advance the field start to become clear.

Embracing new things is never easy. At times, you may feel tempted to just keep things as is. However, when teachers are inspired to try new things and learn new ways, our life can be more efficient, productive, and successful. We simply need to give ourselves the opportunity to change our practices in positive ways.

 **Stop and Jot**

We have provided two models describing how people respond to change over time. For this last Stop and Jot, we suggest taking time to make your own timeline of the highs and lows you have already experienced getting to know, use, and embrace artificial intelligence.

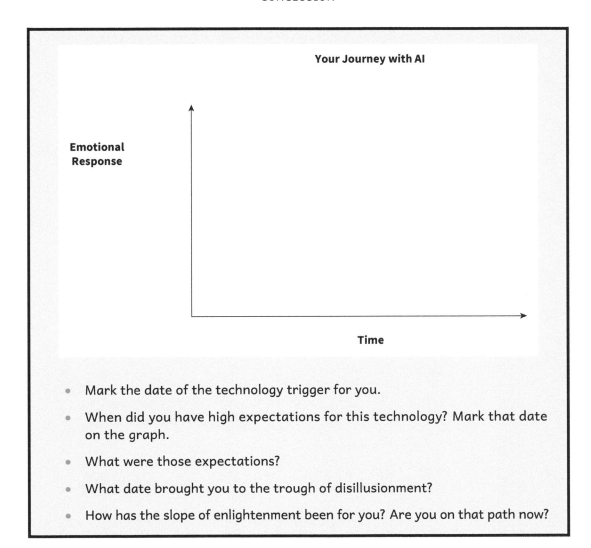

**Your Journey with AI**

Emotional Response

Time

- Mark the date of the technology trigger for you.
- When did you have high expectations for this technology? Mark that date on the graph.
- What were those expectations?
- What date brought you to the trough of disillusionment?
- How has the slope of enlightenment been for you? Are you on that path now?

We hope that you are reaching the plateau of productivity. We want all educators to be able to develop a strong life–work balance, and we believe that AI can help you with some of the required functions that take you away from your direct interactions with students. As you reflect on your experiences with AI, we invite you to engage in another self-assessment. Where are you now with some of the functions that can be supported by AI?

## Self-Assessment

*Where are you now with the use of AI in these essential functions?*

| Using AI for Educator Functions | |
|---|---|
| I can use AI in content generation, content organization, content revision, and content consolidation. | 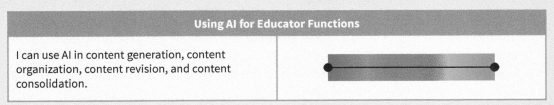 |

*(Continued)*

(Continued)

| Using AI for Educator Functions | |
|---|---|
| I can use AI to increase relevance for students and to engage students in meaningful learning. | |
| I can use AI to help me design instructional experiences. | |
| I can use AI to develop and evaluate or interpret assessments. | |
| I can use AI to help me provide effective, growth-producing feedback for students. | |
| I can use AI in my own learning. | |
| I can integrate AI into my class such that students have opportunities to learn ethical uses of these tools. | |

We ask ChatGPT how to end a book for educators about AI, and here is the response:

*As we close this exploration of AI in education, remember that the future is in your hands. As educators, you are not just witnesses to the evolution of technology; you are architects of its impact on the next generation.*

*Embrace the possibilities that AI brings to the classroom, viewing it not as a replacement for teachers but as a powerful ally. Nurture a mindset of adaptability, curiosity, and continuous learning. Equip your students with the skills to thrive in a world where AI is both a tool and a challenge.*

*In the grand tapestry of education, AI is but one thread. You, the educators, are the weavers, shaping the narrative of the future. Your passion, dedication, and creativity are the driving forces that will determine how AI enhances the educational experience.*

*As you embark on this AI-infused journey, remember that the heart of education remains the same—the connection between teacher and student, the joy of discovery, and the cultivation of critical thinking. Embrace technology, but never lose sight of the human touch that makes education truly transformative.*

*May your classrooms be filled with innovation, compassion, and a commitment to preparing the next generation for a future we can only begin to imagine. The journey is ongoing, and you, dear educators, are the captains guiding the ship into uncharted waters. Here's to a future where AI and education coalesce to create a world of endless possibilities. The adventure continues, and you are at the helm. Happy teaching! (OpenAI, 2023).*

Thank you, ChatGPT, for those wise words. As you continue on your journey, may your classrooms be filled with joy and may your careers be rewarding. You are the critical factor in your students' education—and AI can serve as an effective tool to help you accomplish your goals.

# APPENDIX
# Check-for-Understanding Answers

## CHAPTER 1

Question 1: What does the Kübler-Ross Change Curve, as mentioned in the chapter, aim to capture?

Answer: Emotional response to change

Question 2: What is the primary purpose of large language model (LLM) artificial intelligence tools?

Answer: Generate and create human-like content

Question 3: What is the function of teacher-facing artificial intelligence sites?

Answer: Educator assistant for creating engaging resources and generating content

Question 4: What is the primary audience of this playbook?

Answer: Teachers and leaders

Question 5: What does the term *guardrails* refer to in the context of AI, as mentioned in the chapter?

Answer: Policies or restrictions used to ensure AI handles data responsibly

## CHAPTER 2

Discussion Question #1: What are your concerns about integrating AI into education, particularly in terms of ethical use and avoiding plagiarism? How do you think educators can address these concerns effectively?

Possible Replies:

- This is a technology teachers and students are learning about at the same time, it will be important that teacher use and student use are two things that people take time to learn and teach.

- Increased plagiarism is a concern, to avoid this it is important users know how to responsibly interact with AI tools.

- Educators should work together with colleagues and school to create clear guidelines on ethical AI use.

- This is an opportunity to teach ethical use and critical consumption of content from many platforms, including AI. It is an important thing to teach when there is so much content being shared readily on various online sites.

Discussion Question #2: Considering the guidelines provided for crafting strong prompts for AI, how important do you think it is for educators to master the skill of communicating with AI systems? What potential challenges do you foresee in prompt writing for AI, and how could these be mitigated?

Possible Replies:

- In order to best use these sites, it feels crucial for educators to learn how to obtain the right information.

- If students will learn to write prompts in the future, already something being taught at the higher education level, teachers should also be learning this skill.

- It seems like the better the prompt, the better the output. With this in mind, it is important because we want teachers to know just how helpful AI tools can and will be.

- Having training and time dedicated to learn effective prompt writing and other important skills users of AI need is essential.

Discussion Question #3: How can educators effectively teach students about plagiarism in the context of AI-generated content? What strategies or activities could you employ to ensure students understand the ethical use of AI-generated material and the importance of proper citation and attribution?

Possible Replies:

- It is important to show students examples of content generated solely with AI vs. content generated with human users so that they see the difference and learn how important it is to avoid unethical use of AI tools.

- Teachers should teach students about plagiarism, like they would other classroom skills, and give them time to really learn what it is and how to avoid it.

- Giving students instruction in how to cite the use of AI and modeling citation structures is critical.

## EDUCATOR FUNCTION #1: MANAGING CONTENT

Scenario 1: As a middle school science teacher, you are looking to use AI to help you generate content for a new unit you will be teaching next month. Specifically, you would like help on engaging experiments. How could you use AI to generate creative and innovative ideas for science labs in this unit? What are all the ways you can use AI tools to help? What types of content can it generate to help with the overall teaching experience?

Possible Answer: AI can assist by giving ideas for innovative experiments aimed at practicing a specific standard or scientific concept. Entering a prompt like, "Give ideas for engaging science experiments for middle school students focusing on [topic]," and including details like the duration or available materials for student use, is sure to give some helpful ideas. This teacher could also ask for student directions for the experiment, questions for students to consider when completing the assignment, and even ideas for a formative assessment or check-for-understanding at the end.

Scenario 2: You are a third-grade teacher tasked with integrating content areas with literacy. You decide to integrate social studies with speaking and listening into a cohesive learning experience for students. How would you leverage AI to consolidate content and create a comprehensive lesson that incorporates concepts from both subjects?

Possible Answer: This teacher will want to start by having a clear objective for the skill or content they want students to learn and practice for both social studies and speaking and listening. They can visit a generative AI site, like ChatGPT, and write a prompt that includes both of these goals and a request for lessons or activities that will help third-grade students practice both. For example, "Create a lesson for third-grade students integrating [social studies topic] and [speaking and listening standard]." The teacher can review the results and either use the ideas given as is, or use the ideas given to spark their own idea of what to teach that meets the goal.

Scenario 3: You are an English teacher who has thirteen instructional days before an upcoming break. You are teaching an argument-writing unit and, according to the curriculum resource being used, you have nineteen sessions to teach. How could you use AI to help you arrange this unit in a way that allows you to fit it in before the break? What details will be important to include when seeking assistance from AI?

Possible Answer:

With the unit objectives and essential outcomes in mind, this teacher can ask AI for a few possible plans for how to teach the lessons in a shorter number of days. Using a prompt like, "Help create a plan for the rest of this [topic] writing unit. We have [number of days] and need to cover [essential skill]. Please use some of the objectives in this list [list of content you are trying to fit into this timeframe]," will yield results that will help with a plan. The teacher could continue a back-and-forth with the chatbot until they land on a plan that feels it matches what they are looking for.

# EDUCATOR FUNCTION #2: FOSTERING STUDENT ENGAGEMENT

1. True: AI tools can help teachers with ideas for building student background knowledge and can be used for students to tap into the background knowledge they already have.

2. True: Artificial Intelligence can assist educators in making content more relevant and personalized for individual students.

3. False: Choice boards are primarily used to give students extra work to complete when they finish another assigned task.

4. True: Gaming can be used to make learning enjoyable, memorable, and motivating.

5. False: You should avoid having students use AI to plan for conversations with peers because it will take away from their original ideas.

## EDUCATOR FUNCTION #3: MEETING STUDENTS' INSTRUCTIONAL NEEDS

Question 1: What are the three areas in which educators should consider customizing learning experiences for students?

Answer: Content, process, and product

Question 2: What is one way in which AI can support students with literacy-related disabilities?

Answer: Creating recordings of themselves reading

Question 3: What is the purpose of the "Magic School Text-Leveler Tool" mentioned in the Educator Function?

Answer: To adjust the complexity of texts

Question 4: How can AI help teachers create scaffolds for students?

Answer: By providing lists of sentence starters

Question 5: What is a key consideration when implementing classroom interventions, as mentioned in the Educator Function?

Answer: Thoughtfully designing interventions with a particular learner or group of learners in mind

## EDUCATOR FUNCTION #4: ASSESSING STUDENT LEARNING

1) Assessment is an essential function of teachers and serves as an important factor in connecting _____ and _____.

   Answer: teaching, learning

2) Universal Response assessments are useful for assessing _____ and engaging all students in thinking and _____.

   Answer: understanding, application

3) AI-resistant assessments encourage educators to rethink the nature of tasks and focus on obtaining data points that show the _____ of student understanding, knowledge, and application.

   Answer: depth

4) Assessments of Transfer focus on students' ability to carry learning from one context to another, which is considered the best way to demonstrate _____ of a skill.

Answer: mastery

5) The ability of AI tools to automate essential tasks, such as data interpretation, is described as a significant win for teachers, giving them back _____.

Answer: time

# EDUCATOR FUNCTION #5: PROVIDING EFFECTIVE FEEDBACK

Discussion Question 1: How can AI tools be used to enhance the quality and quantity of actionable feedback that students receive in the classroom?

Possible Replies:

- AI tools can quickly analyze student work and give insights into common challenges or areas for improvement. Teachers would be able to focus more on the discussion and making a plan than having to do the sorting and initial analysis that can often be the most time-consuming.

- AI can help identify patterns in student work that will help teachers make a plan for what to do in response to the feedback.

- When teachers use AI, they are getting a model or other things to say about student work and different types of feedback to give. This could help the user get better at giving feedback themselves with or without AI tools.

Discussion Question 2: What are the potential benefits and limitations of using AI for providing feedback to students, especially in relation to the timeliness and specificity of the feedback?

Possible Replies:

- Benefits: timeliness in giving feedback, feedback that is actionable, feedback based on specific rubric criteria, automate assessment in a way that does not give as much subjectivity as some traditional grading does.

- Limitations: AI doesn't necessarily understand the context of each assignment, the tool does not know background of the student it gives feedback to, lacks the personal touch that teachers bring.

Discussion Questions 3: How might the integration of AI tools in feedback processes influence students' ability to seek and utilize feedback effectively, and what implications does this have for their learning journey and growth mindset?

Possible Replies:

- These tools can provide consistent and objective assessment as students are working through an assignment. It could help them use a rubric throughout the learning process and not just at the end.

- Allows students to seek feedback when they most need it, not having to wait for the next day or an available teacher.

- Promotes the growth mindset in students by teaching them that getting feedback along the way can help make a stronger, and more effective, learning experience.

## EDUCATOR FUNCTION #6: LIFELONG LEARNING

Scenario 1: You are an educator attending a professional development session where you learn about a new teaching approach. How would you utilize AI tools to further understand and adapt this approach to fit your specific classroom needs and student population?

Possible Answer: After learning about new possibilities, using AI to help match the suggestion to the reality of your classroom is a great way to engage with a generative AI tool like ChatGPT. I could prompt the chatbot with a question like, "We just learned how to do [topic]. I am a [grade level or subject] teacher who would like to use this in my classrooms. How can I modify the idea to work in my classroom?" After that, I would back and forth with the chatbot using it to help gain insights, generate ideas, and tailor suggestions that apply to my classroom.

Scenario 2: You are a teacher who needs to clarify a specific topic or concept related to your content area. How would you use AI to engage in a dynamic conversation to gain a deeper understanding tailored to your specific teaching needs?

Possible Answer: AI can be a thought partner, a teacher, and colleague-like tool that can help users better understand many concepts. I would use a Chatbot in this scenario and ask it a prompt like, "Teach me about [topic or content] and give me things I need to know about it that will help me teach [grade level or subject]." I would continue to ask questions to help me grasp the concept, maybe asking for examples or details after the initial output.

Scenario 3: You're a seasoned educator contemplating adjusting your instructional approach to better align with your students' needs. How might AI serve as a valuable resource in teaching you about new activities or teaching methods you can use with this particular group of learners?

Possible Answer: To learn about new ideas, I would give myself some time to explore some of the features of teacher-facing AI sites. If I knew what I wanted to teach but was thinking about how to repackage it, I would look for a tool that matched my vision. I could also go to a general AI site like ChatGPT and ask it to give suggestions for new activities or teaching methods. To do this I might ask, "What teaching methods are effective for teaching [grade level and student demographic] students [topic]?" Perhaps prompting what methods or activities used in the past would ensure the ideas were new and innovative.

# REFERENCES

Berry, A. (2020). Disrupting to driving: Exploring upper primary teachers' perspectives on student engagement. *Teachers and Teaching, 26*(2), 145–165.

Best Review Guide. (2024, January 3). *Best translator earbuds.* https://www.bestreviews.guide/translator-earbuds?

Blubaugh, D. (1999). Bringing cable into the classroom. *Educational Leadership*, 46(5). https://www.ascd.org/el/articles/bringing-cable-into-the-classroom

Fisher, D., & Frey, N. (2018). Raise reading volume through access, choice, discussion, and book talks. *The Reading Teacher, 72*, 89–97.

Fisher, D., Frey, N., & Hattie, J. (2016). *Visible learning for literacy.* Corwin.

Fisher, D., Frey, N., & Hattie, J. (2020). *The distance learning playbook, grades K–12.* Corwin.

Fisher, D., Frey, N., Amador, O., & Assof, J. (2024). *The teacher clarity playbook, grades K-12* (2nd ed.). Corwin.

Fisher, D., Frey, N., Bustamante, V., & Hattie, J. (2020). *The assessment playbook for online and blended learning.* Corwin.

Fisher, D., Frey, N., Ortega, S., & Hattie, J. (2023). *Teaching students to drive their learning: A playbook on engagement and self-regulation.* Corwin.

Frey, N., Fisher, D., & Almarode, J. (2023). *How scaffolding works: A playbook for supporting and releasing responsibility to students.* Corwin.

Green, A. (2015, September 15). *The Yale chalkboard rebellion of 1830.* Mental Floss. https://www.mentalfloss.com/article/68749/yale-chalkboard-rebellion-1830

Guskey, T. R., & Link, L. J. (2022). What teachers really want when it comes to feedback. *Educational Leadership, 79*(7), 42–48.

Hawe, E., Dixon, H., & Hamilton, R. (2021). Why and how educators use exemplars. *Journal of University Teaching & Learning Practice, 18*(3). https://ro.uow.edu.au/jutlp/vol18/iss3/010

Hicks, C. (2023, December 27). What Is the Gartner Hype Cycle? The Gartner Hype Cycle tracks the progression of a new technology as it enters the market. *Money.* https://money.usnews.com/investing/articles/gartner-hype-cycle

IBM Data and AI Team. (2023, October 16). Shedding light on AI bias with real-world examples. *Artificial Intelligence.* https://www.ibm.com/blog/shedding-light-on-ai-biaswith-real-world-examples/

Jung, L. A., Frey, N., Fisher, D., & Kroener, J. (2019). *Your students, my students, our students: Rethinking equitable and inclusive classrooms.* ASCD.

Kahn, S. (2023, May 1). *AI in the classroom can transform education* [Video]. https://blog.khanacademy.org/sal-khans-2023-ted-talk-ai-in-the-classroom-can-transform-education/

Klein, A. (2021, December 6). 1,500 decisions a day (at least!): How teachers cope with a dizzying array of questions. *EducationWeek.* https://www.edweek.org/teaching-learning/1-500-decisions-a-day-at-least-how-teachers-cope-with-a-dizzying-array-of-questions/2021/12

Kraft, N. (2023, December 17). Ross Levinsohn firing is most recent Sports Illustrated embarrassment. *Forbes.* https://www.forbes.com/sites/nicolekraft/2023/12/17/ross-levinsohn-firing-is-most-recent-sports-illustrated-embarrassment/?sh=478dd6f83f01

Lee, I. (2009). Ten mismatches between teachers' beliefs and written feedback practice. *ELT 100 Journal, 63*(1), 13–22.

Liang, H., Wang, X., & An, R. (2023). Influence of Pokémon GO on physical activity and psychosocial well-being in children and adolescents: Systematic review. *Journal of Medical Internet Research, 25,* e49019. https://doi.org/10.2196/49019

Lo, C. K. (2023). What is the impact of ChatGPT on education? A rapid review of the literature. *Education Sciences, 13,* 410. doi: 10.3390/educsci13040410

Marr, B. (2023, May 19). A short history of ChatGPT: How we got to where we are today. *Forbes Magazine.* https://www.forbes.com/sites/bernardmarr/2023/05/19/a-short-history-of-chatgpt-how-we-got-to-where-we-are-today/?sh=4b3636c6674f

McGrath, R. (2023, April 21). *The power of lifelong learning: How curiosity forges mastery.* Forbes Business Council. Forbes Councils Member. https://www.forbes.com/sites/forbesbusinesscouncil/2023/04/21/the-power-of-lifelong-learning-how-curiosity-forges-mastery/

McKinsey & Company. (2020). *McKinsey Global Teacher and Student Survey.* https://www.mckinsey.com/industries/education/our-insights/how-artificial-intelligence-will-impact-k-12-teachers

Naylor, P. R. (1991). *Shiloh.* Bantam Doubleday Dell.

Panadero, E., & Lipnevich, A. A. (2021). A review of feedback models and typologies: Towards an integrative model of feedback elements. *Educational Research Review,* 100416. doi:10.1016/j.edurev.2021.100416

Priniski, S. J., Hecht, C. A., & Harackiewicz, J. M. (2018). Making learning personally meaningful: A new framework for relevance research. *Journal of Experimental Education, 86,* 11–29.

Rasinski, T., & Cheesman Smith, M. (2020). *Daily word ladders: Idioms, grades 4+: 90 word ladders to take word study to the next level.* Scholastic.

Rosenthal, R., & Jacobson, L. (1968). *Pygmalion in the classroom: Teacher expectation and pupils' intellectual development.* Holt, Rinehart & Winston.

Rubie-Davies, C. M. (2007). Classroom interactions: Exploring the practices of high- and low-expectation teachers. *British Journal of Educational Psychology, 77*(2), 289–306.

Rubie-Davies, C., Hattie, J., & Hamilton, R. (2006). Expecting the best for students: Teacher expectations and academic outcomes. *British Journal of Educational Psychology, 76*(3), 429–444.

Saville-Troike, M. (1988). Private speech: Evidence for second language learning strategies, during the "silent period." *Journal of Child Language, 15*(3), 567–590.

Serviss, J. (2022, May 13). *4 Benefits of an active professional learning community.* https://iste.org/blog/4-benefits-of-an-active-professional-learning-community

Shrum, D. (2019). Empower students through individual conferences. *ASCD, 14*(22). https://www.ascd.org/el/articles/empower-students-through-individual-conferences

Simousek, W. (2015, June 29). Differentiation has been going on since the one-room school. *Educational Consultant.* https://www.example website.com/full-article-url

Stanford HAI. (2023, March 8). *AI+Education Summit: Generative AI for Education* [Video]. YouTube. https://www.youtube.com/watch?v=Ks7enkKuZIo

Tomlinson, C. A., & Imbeau, M. (2023). *Leading and managing a differentiated classroom* (2nd ed.). ASCD.

U.S. Department of Education, Office of Educational Technology (2023). *Artificial intelligence and future of teaching and learning: Insights and recommendations.* Author. https://tech.ed.gov

Venkatesh, V., & Davis, F. D. (1996). A model of the antecedents of perceived ease of use: development and test. *Decision Sciences, 27,* 451–481.

Vosen, M. A. (2008). Using Bloom's taxonomy to teach students about plagiarism. *The English Journal, 97*(6), 43–46.

WeberWulff, D., AnohinaNaumeca, A., Bjelobaba, S., Foltýnek, T., GuerreroDib, J., Popoola, O., Šigut, P., & Waddington, L. (2023). Testing of detection tools for AI-generated text. *International Journal for Educational Integrity, 19*(26). https://doi.org/10.1007/s40979-023-00146-z

Will, M. (2023, December 15). The teaching profession in 2023 (in charts). *EducationWeek.* https://www.edweek.org/teaching-learning/the-teaching-profession-in-2023-in-charts/2023/

Wisniewski, B., Zierer, K., & Hattie, J. (2020). The power of feedback revisited: A meta-analysis of educational feedback research. *Frontiers in Psychology, 10,* 3087. https://doi.org/10.3389/fpsyg.2019.03087

# INDEX

academic topics, 116
adjustments, 62, 69, 71, 76–77
AI-generated content, 23, 28–29, 32, 34, 60, 136
AI-Resistant Assessments, 90–91, 95, 138
analysis of student assessment data, 94
application, 20, 29, 39, 86, 90–91, 93, 95, 138
    real-world, 88, 90
artificial intelligence sites, 12, 32
    teacher-facing, 16, 21, 135
assessment development, 83
assessment questions, 46
assessments, multiple-choice, 46, 91
assessment techniques, 87, 89
assessment tools, 44, 83, 86, 90–91
assessment types, common, 87
attendance, 11, 38
Audiopen.ai, 19, 72–73

background knowledge, 39, 42, 49, 51, 64–65,
    121, 137
    building student, 64, 137
balance, 89, 98
biases, 15, 20, 23, 32

chains, 120
chalkboards, 1–2, 129
chatbot, 17, 20, 51, 53–54, 56–57, 59, 61, 63, 67,
    85, 99, 104, 116–17, 119–20, 140
ChatGPT, 2, 4, 11, 13, 15, 16, 18, 23, 27, 28, 31,
    33, 42, 46, 60, 79, 86, 93, 103-108, 111,
    122-123, 132, 133, 137, 140
choice boards, 19, 40, 57–59, 64, 125, 138
classification levels, 33
classmate, 71–72, 93, 102
classroom assessments, 85, 95
clickup.com/blog/ai-tools-forstudents, 72
coach, 78, 112–13
coach students, 94, 113
comprehension question, 89, 94
computer, 4, 17, 20, 24
concepts, 28–29, 31, 38, 40, 46–47, 75, 77–78, 90,
    92, 97–98, 120, 125, 128, 137, 140

conferences, 3, 103, 115
consolidate content, 43–44, 47, 137
content
    customize, 69, 75
    generated, 17, 33
    generating, 21, 40, 135
    human-like, 21, 135
content area, 47, 93, 117–19, 127–28,
    137, 140
content consolidation, 39, 43, 131
content creation, 45, 47
content generation, 39–40, 131
content knowledge, 74, 115
content organization, 39, 41–42, 131
content revision, 39, 42, 131
continuum, 53, 62–63
conversations
    dynamic, 119–20, 128, 140
    tool transcribes group, 72
credibility, 23, 31–34, 80
criteria, 30–31, 38–39, 76, 84
cues, 20, 24, 41, 63–64, 77, 112
customize, 49, 60, 65, 67, 81, 84

decisions, 2, 4, 10, 14, 41, 70, 83–84, 121
deliverables, 33
description, 26, 44, 72–73
detection tools educators, 28
dialogue, 14, 26, 34
digital tools, 28, 119
disillusionment, 130–31

Eduaide.ai, 16–17, 19, 58, 79, 125, 127
educator assistant, 21, 135
educators change content, 53
educators reimagine assessment, 85
emotional response, 9, 21–22, 135
engagement, 5, 49, 55, 57, 59, 62–64
English teachers, 47, 101, 137
enlightenment, 130–31
exemplars, 44, 71–72, 102, 109–10
expertise, 86, 100

feedback
  actionable, 97, 114, 139
    growth-producing, 132
    real-time, 98, 112
feedback content, 114
feedback models, 101–2
feedback processes influence students, 114, 139
feedback style, 102
fluency, 61, 121–23
format, 25–26, 39, 87–88, 109, 111
fractions, 40, 42

games, 3, 12, 59, 90
Google, 13–14, 18, 72, 119
Google Classroom, 17–19
Google search, 13–14, 51, 57, 116, 119
graders, 3–4, 74, 109, 120, 122
grade students, 30, 40, 46
graphic organizers, 77–78
growth-producing feedback for students, 132
guide students, 29, 43, 103, 115

high-expectation practices, 70–71
highlight, 76, 100–101, 112
human users, 20, 30–32, 40, 45, 136

IEPs (individual education programs), 72
images, 19–20, 72, 75
individual education programs (IEPs), 72
input, 12–13, 17, 20, 24–25, 76–77, 79,
    94, 103
interests, 49–51, 53–55, 59, 65, 70, 81
interventions, 61, 78–81, 92

Kübler-Ross Change Curve, 10, 21, 129, 135

languages, 30, 66, 74–75
learners, 49, 53–55, 57, 62, 65–66, 68–69, 71,
    74–76, 78, 81, 90, 92–93, 103, 138, 140
    lifelong, 115–16, 128
    multilingual, 74–75
length, 25, 41, 109
lesson plans, 21, 44–45, 80, 118, 124
letters, 60–61, 93–94
lifelong learning, 115–16, 127, 140
limitations, 16, 29–30, 32, 88, 114, 139
LLM (large language models), 12–13, 18,
    20–21, 135

MagicSchool.ai, 2, 16–17, 19, 54–55, 58, 64, 68,
    90, 110, 125, 127
middle school science teacher, 38, 47, 136
middle school students, 79, 137

peer feedback, 87, 102, 112–13
peer responses, 71
phrases, 20, 25–26, 30, 44, 75
plagiarism, 5, 23, 27–29, 34, 136
plan instruction, 86, 129
plateau, 130–31
PLCs (professional learning community), 71
productive coaching, 108–9
professional learning, 115, 118–19
proficiency, 33, 76, 93, 109
prompts, 23–33, 113

relevance, 5, 14, 49, 53–56, 64, 86, 132
reprompt, 41, 44, 61
responses, 13, 15, 17, 24–26, 30–31, 33–34,
    78, 88, 90, 94–95, 99–100, 103, 105, 107–9,
    131–32
responsibility, 2, 14, 33, 37, 40, 65, 80, 97
risks, 4, 15, 67, 78, 81
rubric, 38–39, 43, 76, 87, 139

scaffolding, 77–78
scaffolds, 66, 69, 77–78, 80, 138
scenario, 47, 66, 86–87, 92–93, 127–28,
    136–37, 140
scenario-based questions, 21, 127
schools, middle, 3, 57, 61
script, 61
search engines, 4, 13–14, 21
seasoned educator, 128, 140
simulation, 93–94
site www.magicschool.ai, teacher-facing, 77
skills and tools, 115
skills students, 59, 84, 122
Socrat.ai, 17–19, 51–53, 121, 125, 127
specificity, 25, 45, 97, 103, 114, 139
standards, grade-level, 109
story, 26, 40, 61, 89
student assessment data, 94
student conferences, 102–3, 108
student conversations, 19, 51
student engagement, 5, 53, 56, 61–62, 124
student essay, 38
student learners, 103
student population, 69, 128, 140
students' ability to transfer skills and
    knowledge, 92
students content, 61
students feedback, 12, 99–100, 102,
    109, 124
student tools, 72
student users, 113
support student engagement, 56

surface, 3, 92
synthesize student responses, 3

teacher-facing sites, 16, 68, 72
teacher-facing tools support, 86
teacher function, 19, 39
teachers, 1–5, 16–17, 19, 30–31, 37–39, 51, 54–57, 62–69, 74, 76–81, 83–85, 87–89, 92–99, 101–3, 109–10, 112–15, 118–22, 124–25, 128–30, 135–40
  fourth-grade, 16, 121, 123
  grade, 25, 118
  kindergarten, 94
  sixth-grade, 71, 94
  support, 5, 95, 118
  third-grade, 47, 109, 137
teachers feedback, 99, 124
teaching students, 28, 34, 43, 45–46, 63, 113
teaching tools, 124–25
technology teachers, 135
third-grade level, 26
third-grade students, 26, 42, 137
time constraints, 2, 39, 42
time educators, 114
timeframes, 41, 137
timeline, 19, 28, 122, 130
timeliness, 97, 100, 114, 139
time teachers, 5

tips, 45–46, 111, 113
tools
  artificial intelligence, 21, 135
  collaboration, 118–19
  communication, 30, 72
  higher-end technology, 11
  plagiarism detection, 28
  self-assessment, 70
  teacher-facing, 103
  technological, 45
  technology-based, 38
tools for content creation, 45
tools for educators, 15
tools for students, 72–73, 87
tools in action, 21, 74
tools in feedback, 114, 139
tools to automate, 94–95, 139
track, 19, 38, 89, 94
transfer, 17, 92–93
translation, 74–75
true/false questions, 21, 86
trust, 31, 33, 93

verification, 32–33
vocabulary, 41, 59–61, 74–76, 92
voice, 30–31, 43, 75, 77, 103, 111

Wikipedia, 32
Word Ladder Game, 60–61

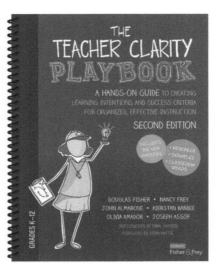
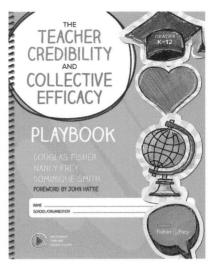

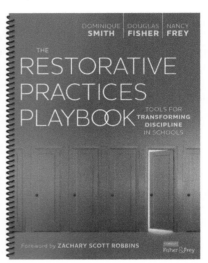

## AI in Education: Your Path to Tomorrow's Classroom with Corwin Professional Learning

Designed for district leaders and educators, Corwin offers PD opportunities that are built to meet your goals. You'll dive into the world of Artificial Intelligence (AI) in the classroom through our interactive events and courses, led by Corwin experts.

- Delve deeper into practical strategies outlined in the Artificial Intelligence Playbook.

- Walk away equipped with impactful practices that you can implement as soon as tomorrow.

Scan to get details

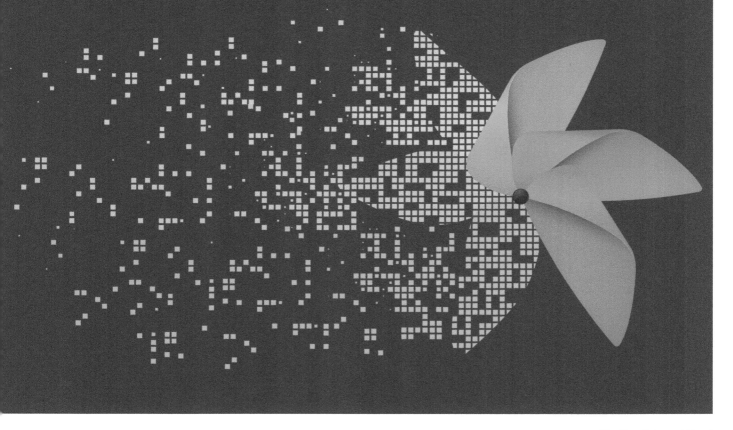

CORWIN

**A Sage Company**

**CORWIN HAS ONE MISSION:** to enhance education through intentional professional learning.

We build long-term relationships with our authors, educators, clients, and associations who partner with us to develop and continuously improve the best evidence-based practices that establish and support lifelong learning.